Acting in Prime Time

The Mature Person's Guide to Breaking into Show Business

Terry Chayefsky

Heinemann
Portsmouth, NH

Heinemann
A division of Reed Elsevier Inc.
361 Hanover Street
Portsmouth, NH 03801-3912

Offices and agents throughout the world

The author and publisher wish to thank those who have generously given permission to reprint material: Dolly Sloan photo by David M. Brown. Joan Lowry photo by Bill Morris. Frank Nugent photo © Benn Mitchell. Bea DeLizio photo by Roy Blakey. Larry O'Brien photo by Joe Henson, NYC. Stephen Lewis photo by Amy Ward/Award Agency. Bill Bowdren photo by Glenn Jussen, Jussen Studio. Patricia Veliotes photo by John Hart. Patti Karr photo from Portraits by Chuck Karel. Nella Griffin photo by Eric Stephen Jacobs.

Library of Congress Cataloging-in-Publication Data
Chayefsky, Terry.
    Acting in prime time : the mature person's guide to breaking into show business / Terry Chayefsky.
      p. cm.
    Includes bibliographical references.
    ISBN 0-435-07011-8
      1. Acting—Vocational guidance—United States. 2. Career changes—United States. I. Title.
    PN2055.C437   1996
    792'.02'93—dc20   96-27003
                                   CIP

Editor: Lisa A. Barnett
Production: Vicki Kasabian
Book design: Mary C. Cronin
Cover design: Jenny Jensen Greenleaf
Manufacturing: Louise Richardson
Printed in the United States of America on acid-free paper
99 98 97 96 DA 1 2 3 4 5

To Emma, Eric, Carson, Kali, and Noah,
who fill my life with sweetness.
And to Harvey, who's "a hell of a fella."

Contents

Acknowledgments

I want to express my gratitude to the people who have shared their knowledge and experiences with me. I sincerely hope that I have given them sufficient credit in the body of this book.

I also would like to express my appreciation to my children—Amy, Guy, Harold, and Kim—for their encouragement and support and for initiating me into the mysteries of the world of the computer. Thanks, too, to Heidi Silverstone, my computer guru.

Additionally, I want to honor my debt to Lenore Perlmutter, Steven Kaye, and Susan Wishnow for additional data on people over fifty.

I also want to thank Lisa Barnett, my editor, for her constructive suggestions and her upbeat attitude, which enhanced the pleasure of writing this book.

And a special thanks to my dear friend and companion, Dr. Harvey E. Kaye, for his patience, support, and editorial wisdom.

1

Opportunities for a Unique Second Career

Does a second chance appeal to you? One that would contribute to your enjoyment, enhance your life style, and provide satisfaction and a paycheck to boot? Dreams sometimes do come true. A fact of modern life is that second careers and two-job families have become institutional in our culture.

There is a segment of the world of show business where advertising and entertainment overlap, and it welcomes mature people. The environment is one of creativity, recognition, and interesting relationships with talented people. Moreover, the potential for earning additional income always looms in the background. This segment encompasses

1. Modeling for print ads in magazines, newspapers, brochures, flyers, and other publications;
2. Working as an extra in films, soaps, and television; and
3. Acting as a principal in commercials.

In this uncertain world lie untold possibilities. (Occasionally, little acorns do grow into spectacular trees.)

The total package is a triad consisting of print work, extra work, and commercials. You can participate in all three, concentrate on two, or specialize in one. You can pursue this part- or full-time, depending on your needs and inclinations. Working on a scene in a movie, a segment on a soap, a commercial, or an ad for a magazine, you can become part of a profession viewed by millions of people (on the screen and in print), including your family and friends. Another plus is that the work is more colorful and creative than the average nine-to-five job, and so are the people you work with.

Let me use myself as an example. At age fifty-five, I took early retirement from my job as a speech therapist with the Westchester school system in Rye, New York. My family was grown, I had lots of energy, and I decided to seize the moment to try another profession.

I wanted to do work that would provide satisfaction, suppliment my pension, be interesting, and yet not be a nine-to-five job. I had always loved the theater and movies, and this was my dream: to be part of the world of show business. However, I had no idea how to begin to find avenues that would get me into the field. I just wanted to be part of the business. It took years to learn what I now want to share with you.

To date, I've done commercials, extra work, a plethora of print modeling, and soaps, including *As the World Turns* and *One Life to Live,* in which I've appeared many times. I've also appeared in many movies, working with Tom Hanks, Anne Meara, Sean Penn, Robert De Niro, Dustin Hoffman, Barbra Streisand, Harrison Ford, Robin Williams, Martin Landau, Brian Dennehy, Alexis Smith, Woody Allen, Mia Farrow, and Sidney Pollack, just to name a few. It's a fantastic industry, and there is always that wonderful sense of excitement and camaraderie that few other fields seem to offer.

This field has no age limit. You can work 'til you're one hundred. (It's not the age, it's the condition.) Florence McGee, a commercial actress from South Florida, started doing commercials in her eighties. Now, at ninety-two, the only concession she makes to the passage of time is to have a car pick her up and drive her to and from her shoots.

At this writing, she has several commercials running. One is for the Lotto game; another is for Berwick Car Dealers. In the Berwick commercial, she's one of two women sitting on a bench. The other woman boasts about her son the doctor. Florence comes back with the line, "My son drives a car from Berwick." She loves it when people stop her in the street and say things like, "How's your son doing?"

Advertisers salivate for people with whom the mature public can identify, personalities who can sell their products and make

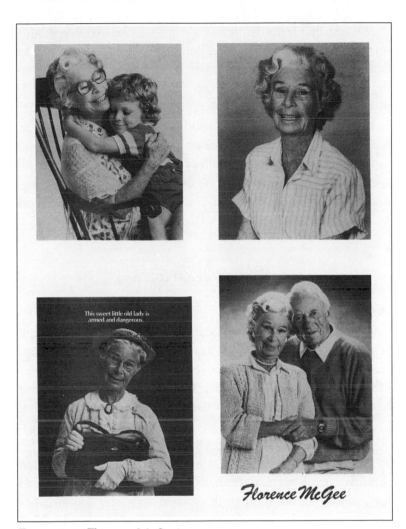

This sweet little old lady is armed and dangerous.

Florence McGee

Figure 1–1. Florence McGee's composite

it believable. They might want *you* for commercials and print: they might want your face—with the imprint of your life experience on it—to sell their products. Obviously, you would seem more convincing than a younger person when you take the pill that takes away the pain, the depression, or the arthritis. These products need your kind of looks, your knowledge, and your mature approach.

Wilford Brimley, a mature actor who looks like everybody's uncle, recently aired in a cereal commercial for Quaker Oats. In commercials for Scope mouthwash, Procter and Gamble has used older people to show that they can be as reluctant to offer a good-morning kiss before rinsing as yuppie couples are. Etc., etc., etc.

For extra work, television producers and moviemakers use *real people* to enhance the authenticity of their programs and films. They need extras to reflect our society. They want all ages, and the mature extra certainly represents a significant segment of the population. As this book will show, second careers and show business mesh very well.

Why Work Now?

Being Creative

The most creative and satisfactory period of your life may well begin at fifty or later. Anyone can be a late bloomer. The fifty-year-old today is equivalent to a thirty-five-year-old at the beginning of the century; people are living longer and have better health at older ages. Note that the extra time gained in longevity should not be added to the *end* of life but to the *middle*—a period calculated to be roughly ages fifty to seventy-five.

Linda Bronte, a veteran researcher in the field of aging, has recently completed a study that found that most of the people interviewed started their peak of creativity after age fifty. For example, Janet Jeppson-Asimov, sixty-eight, was a practicing psychiatrist for much of her adult life. In her late-fifties, she shut down her medical practice to devote herself full-time to writing. She recently published her nineteenth book. Similarly magazine editor Norman Cousins turned a near-fatal illness into an opportunity, later writing a widely read book titled *Anatomy of an Illness*. At sixty-four he joined the University of California at Los Angeles medical faculty. Cousins died in 1990 at the age of seventy-four.

Another shining example is a show called *Fabulous Palm Spring Follies*, which is currently playing to rave reviews in Palm

Springs, California. It features a cast of dancers aged fifty and over. Mr. Riff Markowitz, the producer, felt that to stage the *Follies* convincingly he would need people who at least had been touched by the era when the *Ziegfeld Follies* flourished. People under fifty, no matter how skilled, could never replicate the glamour of that era.

To date, more than three hundred thousand people have paid thirty dollars per seat to see the *Follies* since it opened at the Plaza Theater in 1992. The show is vital, vibrant, and even sexy, and it seems poised to run as long as the performers last. Anyone expecting either a geriatric act or some golden grandmas will probably be disappointed. A *New York Times* reviewer said, "One needs a ringside seat to see even the slightest sign of age, which could not be detected in either attitudes or their footwork." The dancers do as many as ten shows a week. Nothing seems to trip them up or slow them down.

A unanimous response from the *Follies* girls is that they are all there for the same reason: to prove there's life after fifty.

Making Money

Money may not be everything, but it is a good reason people go into a second career. Often the specific reasons vary:

- Many people are being forced out of their jobs (corporate downsizing, government tightening, loss of business, etc.).
- It is becoming increasingly difficult to be able to manage on one income.
- The additional income enables you to keep the principal of capital investments intact.
- The money allows you to travel and buy nonessentials.
- The extra income provides the thrill of feeling successful and productive.

In addition, many people need to support others; if you can make extra money, it helps. A sixty-five-year-old actress uses the money she earns to contribute to the support of her ninety-year-old mother.

You also may want to earmark your earnings for a hobby. One male model I met lays aside money to buy model airplanes.

Keeping Productive

Other actors come into the business because they have worked at the same job for twenty years and can't face another fifteen or twenty years of doing the same thing. James Cole, a New York actor, practiced dentistry for twenty-five years. He longed for a change. At this writing, James is pursuing an acting career and is again excited about life.

Some grandparents take up second careers to avoid becoming full-time baby-sitters for their working sons and daughters or to get away from the demands of other family members. Some couples find working is good for family life because it gives spouses some relief from each other. But for many, the reason to work is just the opposite. Some older people find working together brings them closer to their lifelong mates. Ruth and Irving Nadler, who are in their eighties, always book jobs as a couple. They find working together enhances their relationship, gives them lots of laughs, and prompts interesting discussions after a day's shoot.

Many actors in their second career find that working keeps them young, wards off senility and mental degeneration, and protects them from boredom. Larry O'Brien was a horse trainer and breeder for thirty-two years. He retired to Puerto Rico in 1993. While he was there, a number of things happened, including boredom with retirement, a hurricane, and a big loss in his life. He watched a great deal of television and saw countless older men doing commercials. "I felt I too could have a future in show business," he says. Larry moved to New York and landed his first national commercial after only eighteen months in the business. Now Larry's busy developing his career, making new friends, and meeting lots of people. He's forgotten what the word *boredom* means.

On a broader note, you may think of a job as the best way to be part of the world, to not be alone, to keep in touch with the "real world," to maintain youthful contacts, to know "what's going on," to stay involved. Bill Bowdren retired four years ago. Now he's a working model in his second career. He explains, "Modeling affects my life. I'm in good shape. It keeps me interested in today's world. In most cases they are looking for people who are with it. You can be old, but you should know what's going on." Bill adds, "People I meet in the business are always interesting; I always feel I walk away enriched. I'm working often, earning money, I take good care of myself. . . . My life is full." Bill has seen men looking in a store window not seeing anything, losing interest in the world. He says, "That could be me. Instead, modeling puts me in touch with myself. It's a great time. A wild day for the next twenty years."

You may continue to work because you think that productive work is good in itself above and beyond the pay, a personal satisfaction. Many continue to work because they say they are "too young to sit around doing nothing," and even those who say they are working primarily for money often add that they would continue to work even if they didn't need to. Like them, you may continue to work because you enjoy the work.

Do I Qualify?

I'm not referring to superstars, supermodels, or lead actors in this book (although in this business anything can happen). So for beginning qualifications, I'd say you are an ideal candidate if you

1. Are well motivated;
2. Have perseverance and a positive attitude;
3. Are reliable and responsible;
4. Have a desire to be part of an exciting profession; and
5. Have a professional approach (that's where this book comes in).

Take Peg Phillips, who portrayed Ruth Ann on *Northern Exposure*. In her first career, Peg was a housewife, mother, and grandmother. At age sixty-five she took a drama course at the University of Washington. She worked as an extra, did some commercials, and was spotted for *Northern Exposure*, where she was given a bit part. However, because of her life experience and training, she became a regular on the program.

Although study in the field is generally recommended, you don't always need formal training to succeed. I've met actors who in their first careers were dentists, doctors, homemakers, stockbrokers, city employees, construction workers, business owners, salespersons, etc. They have chosen acting as their second career, and they love it.

Bill Sturgis, a fireman, was injured and had to retire. Dancing and running were out, but otherwise he remained an active man who was raring to go. When he thought about the option of a second career, he considered the production end of show business. But in the film school where he took some courses, they needed some volunteers to act in the student films. As a mature person, Bill found himself in demand. He discovered that he enjoyed acting very much and that many of his life experiences came in handy for acting. Consequently, he felt encouraged to come into the business as a performer.

Bill didn't have an acting background or knowledge, and he knew no other performers. He tried to find out how and whom to contact, but this took a great deal of time. (He didn't have this book.) By trial and error and a great amount of endurance, Bill *has* been quite successful. He's done extra work and has had speaking roles in a large number of major films, including Woody Allen's *Hannah and Her Sisters*. He worked with Jason Robards and was on *Law and Order* many times. He was often seen on *Saturday Night Live*, *Guiding Light*, *All My Children*, *Ryan's Hope*, and *One Life to Live*, has been a stand-in for Brian Dennehy, and much more. He loves the work, is quite successful, and will probably work for years to come.

Returning to the Business

During the 1980s, Carole Lavin, a middle-aged businesswoman, was doing public relations for textile design and furniture companies. She had done some print work in the 1960s, and in 1991 she came back into the business. Since then Carole has done some commercials (including one for Weight Watchers) and some extra work in soaps and films. "At this stage of my life I have a better understanding of who I am as a person," she says. "I'm more open, I'm surprising myself. I'm a happy person. I'm not stressed out, because I love what I'm doing."

Having a Dream

Like many other performers, Muriel Gould had a dream. After her divorce in 1982, she knew she had to work. Muriel weighed all of her possibilities (things she could do, would do, wanted to do) with the rest of her life. She was fifty-two years old. Then it occurred to her that the opportunity to work again was a gift. She had done community theater, and now her dream of acting could be realized. Muriel knew she would have to do other work to supplement her acting career, but show business was where she wanted to be. Since then she has done   and still does— extra work, commercials, print ads, and a vast amount of theater. Muriel enjoys every job she does, and she feels her life is truly enriched.

The agents and casting directors with whom I've spoken welcome mature people. The jobs are there, despite what can be a great deal of competition (probably less with an older crowd). Don't be discouraged; some people work more than others because of choice, talent, training, being at the right place at the right time, typecasting, or just plain luck.

How you perceive this career and how far you want to go with it are up to you. I can make you aware of the opportunities, tell you whom to contact, help you begin, and guide you through. The rest is up to you. I wish you good luck. I'll be looking for you in the movies, on the tube, and in the print ads.

9

2

The Business of Show Business

There's an old theatrical maxim: show business is 5 percent show and 95 percent business. The professional understands this and prospers, while the dilettante neglects the business and pays the price. It matters not how often you work nor how minimal your role may be. There are tools of the trade that you must have: your photo, résumé, answering device, record keeping skills, and you!

The Photograph

According to another maxim, "A picture is worth a thousand words." Therefore it behooves you to investigate your choices thoroughly, become an educated consumer, and spend the time and money to make your photographs a worthwhile investment. They are, after all, your calling card, as well as your personal ad for your career.

What Kind of Photo Do I Need?

You need a good commercial black-and-white headshot that looks exactly like you, when you are looking good. It should be positive, pleasant, and capture your personality. Above all, it should look animated.

Can I Use a Friend Who Takes Excellent Pictures?

No, unless your friend is a professional photographer who specializes in headshots for professional performers and knows what is needed in the field. Arthur Cohen, a New York photographer, zeroes in with, "There's a big difference between the mantel and the marketplace."

Actors waste money by trying to save money on photos. Most experiences with nonprofessional headshot photographers (and even some professionals) prove disappointing and generally have to be redone. This can be both time-consuming and expensive. I can't guarantee you a perfect headshot, but I can prescribe a formula that generally works.

Locating a Photographer

Most cities have professional headshot photographers who specialize in photos for performers. The best sources for finding a photographer are recommendations from your local model agency (check with several), schools that teach acting in commercials, mature actors whose headshots look good, your local SAG office (see Appendix C), and the trade publications.

Call at least three photographers before you make your first appointment. Tell the photographer you want a black-and-white commercial headshot, and ask these seven basic questions:

1. Does your portfolio include mature people?
2. How much do you charge?
3. How many rolls of film do you shoot?
4. How many exposures are in each roll?
5. Does the price include negatives? If negatives are not included how much are additional 8" x 10" prints?
6. Does the price include a hairstylist and makeup artist?
7. How much do you charge for retouching, if necessary?

After your questions have been answered, make appointments to see the photographers' portfolios before you hire one.

The Appointment Meeting the photographer is of prime importance. Does he or she make you smile? Bring out your personality? Do you feel comfortable and relaxed? If you feel tension or stress, it will show; photos don't lie. If you don't feel exactly right about the photographer, you may be wasting time and money.

As you examine a photographer's portfolio, make sure the photos are sharply focused, not grainy. Look for good contrast between background and subject. Note particularly the photos of mature people. See if the photographer has caught a warm, appealing look. Does the photo project a definite personality?

Nick Granito, who has been a headshot photographer for twenty years, gives the following advice: "You should have good rapport with the photographer so that he or she can pull out the real you."

The Cost The average cost of a quality, professional photographer generally runs from two hundred to four hundred dollars. That price usually includes three rolls of black-and-white film (approximately one hundred and eight shots), three contact sheets (8" x 10" sheets with thirty-six small pictures on them), and two unretouched 8" x 10" prints.

The Photo Session
After you have selected your headshot photographer, arrange for a photo session.

The Consultation Most photographers will want to schedule a consultation about a week before the actual shoot. This appointment may be made at the same time you book your session. The consultation is included in the cost and is well worth the time invested.

Talk about your interests (print modeling, film work, commercials). It's quite helpful for the photographer to know on what area you are going to concentrate. Discuss your clothing (colors, style, number of changes). Find out what takes place during the session. Talk about what the photographer expects of you and what his or her role will be. Nick Granito says, "I expect you to know who you are. From there I can direct and help package you."

Glen Jussen, another New York photographer, believes that the more you know about your physical type, becoming clothing, and flattering colors and your goals in show business, the better prepared you are to take better photos. And the more *you* know about the session, the more comfortable you will feel.

Before you leave the consultation, reconfirm price and product. Check out your hair and makeup options. (Most photographers prepare men at no charge, but suggest that women have a makeup artist, which usually costs fifty to seventy-five dollars. Since most mature women wear their hair short, it generally is not necessary to have a hairdresser.)

Preparing for the Session Preparing for your session physically as well as psychologically is critical but often overlooked. It's best to be at your most comfortable weight. Photographer Arthur Cohen says, "With lighting I can thin you down or fatten you up, but it's better if you do this naturally." Another bit of advice is to make the extra effort to take care of yourself in the days or, even better, the weeks before the session (if you still menstruate, don't schedule the shot for those days). Drink lots of water, avoid alcohol and excess salt, get plenty of sleep, exercise, and proper nutrition. This can only help your photo session.

Make sure your hair is cut to the length that is most flattering, but note that it is not advisable to get a haircut just before a photo session. Let your new "do" grow in for a couple of days to make it more natural. For the mature male, gray or balding hair can be a plus. Make sure your hair is neat and, again, looks exactly you. Here are a few more tips:

- Don't try to cover your age lines — this could be your ticket to success.
- Choose your wardrobe carefully. Dress conservatively. Don't wear anything that will date you—both prints and patterns are out. No black or white. Don't wear a hat, jewelry, or any article of clothing that will draw attention away from your face. Do wear soft, solid colors and incorporate the suggestions of the photographer.
- Get plenty of rest the night before.
- Have your clothes in a garment bag packed and ready to go ahead of time so you're not rushed.
- Arrive early for the session.
- Don't schedule much else for the day.

Day of the Session A number of Polaroids are taken, which gives the photographer a sense of how best to photograph you. It also gives you an opportunity to preview the photographer's work and make any suggestions. Once the shoot begins, the photographer will direct you through various poses, changes of clothing, and facial expressions and will help you to be at ease. (My photographer put on a tape of soft background music while we were shooting. It really was soothing.) The best advice most photographers give is to relax and have fun.

After the Photo Session About a week after the session, the photographer will send you the contact sheets. Your job is to choose the best ones to be enlarged. You will be looking at one hundred and eight tiny pictures of yourself. Examine each picture with a magnifying glass and select the two or three that you think are best. Check the eyes first, then the smile. If you are unsure of which shot to get enlarged, ask people in the business for their opinion. (Family and friends not in the business are usually not good sources of advice.) Ultimately, the decision is yours, *you* have to feel good about sending these pictures out.

Don't have the photographer make duplicate glossies; it will be much too costly. The negatives remain the property of the photographer. Your pictures are used to promote and enhance your career. Only if you submit your photograph for publication in a magazine or newspaper will you need written permission from the photographer, who will supply a photo credit. Just take the photos you decide on and have them mass-produced at a photo reproduction house.

What Should I Ask For? A quality photograph looks professional and shows the actor to his or her best advantage. I would suggest a matte finish with no borders. Have your name printed on the bottom in an easy-to-read type on the lower right- or left-hand corner. Your headshot should serve you long and well. At this stage of our lives we don't change that much. However, I would not recommend having your résumé printed on the back of your photo. Since you will want to add the jobs you do as you work, a separate résumé that you glue or staple to the back of your headshot would certainly be more practical.

Joan D. Lowry

Figure 2–1. A typical headshot

How Many Photos Should I Have Duplicated? One hundred 8" x 10" matte finish prints would be a good beginning to carry you through several mailings and follow-ups. In checking a few good-quality reproduction houses, I found the average prices to be $70 for 50, $90 for 100, $125 for 150. This generally includes having the name printed on the photo.

James Cole

Figure 2–2. Another example of a headshot

The Résumé

In the same way that a good, clear photograph is vital, a good, clear, easy-to-read résumé is essential. No matter how much or how little experience you have, you can create a résumé that looks professional and to the point. Beginners' résumés will necessarily be very brief. That's okay; everybody has to start somewhere. As you work, your résumé will grow.

It is a given that résumés should be accurately typed. It's

worth having it done professionally if you have any doubt about your typing skills. List the information on your résumé by category. Start with your vital statistics and your experience and training, then list any special skills or abilities you might have (see sample résumé and prototype in Figures 2–3 and 2–4).

Vital Statistics

Tell the truth. Don't claim credits you don't have. After your name, include your real height, weight, hair color, eye color, and so on. If you don't want to list your age, you may want to give a realistic age range (fifty to sixty, sixty-five to seventy, over sixty-five). Including your social security number is also very important. You will need it every time you book a job. Finally, make sure you list a correct telephone number or numbers.

Experience and Training

Include your education and any degree you have as well as your first career (nursing, used-car salesman, policeman, waitress, homemaker, etc.). Mention any community or organizational work that might be pertinent. Don't neglect to list college and community theater credits, and if you are taking or have taken an acting course or a course in TV commercials, include that too.

Special Skills

Special skills have been the open sesame for many beginners. But don't claim abilities unless you are good at them (gardening, golf, Ping-Pong, cooking, drawing, etc.). Be sure to include any special attributes, talents, or abilities that would be helpful in casting you. For example, the actor who actually wears dentures or experiences insomnia may well be suited to authentically portray the sufferer who benefits from the advertised product. Advertisers shun false advertising. They try to get some degree of authenticity into their commercials. Authentic foreign accents are worth money too. Even a driver's license can get you work, so list all your assets.

Should you still draw a blank and there is nothing in your past, I would suggest preparing a very neatly typewritten 8" x 10"

	Nellie Newstar

Nellie Newstar

SAG - AFTRA

SS: 092-18-2869

212-570-2704
212-219-0700

Ht: 5'7"
Wt: 135
Hair: Honey brown
Eyes: Blue/green
Age range: 50–65

COMMERCIALS: List upon request

TELEVISION: "One Life to Live" (Guest, Reporter,
Disciple, Nurse)
"As the World Turns" (Juror)
"The Clinic" (Social Worker)
"Law and Order" (Russian Woman)

FILMS: *Prince of Tides*; *Billy Bathgate*; *Bonfire of the Vanities*; *Fair Play* (Mrs. Siren); *Tongs* (Mrs. Lowell)

PRINT: List upon request

THEATER: *The Silver Cord* (Mrs. Phelps); Scenes from *'Night, Mother* (Mother); *The Brothers Karamazov* (Mrs. Khakhakov); *Spoon River Anthology* (Dora Williams)

TRAINING: Theatre: H.B. Studio (Ed Moorehouse),
Geraldine Page Studio (Gerry Page)
Commercials: Joan See, Wendy Dillon
Improvisation: Christine Farrell, SAG
Conservatory

SPECIAL SKILLS: Administrator, Gardener, Teacher, Potter,
Speech Therapist, Gourmet Cook, Mother,
Grandmother

UNIFORMS: Complete nurse's uniform. Seasonal formal gowns. Business suits. Good upscale and casual wardrobe.

Figure 2–3. Sample résumé

Name   Height:
Telephone #   Weight:
                                        Hair:
                                        Eyes:
                                        Age range:

<u>Theater</u> (Film, school, community—omit, if no experience)

<u>Education</u>

<u>Training</u>

<u>Special Talent & Abilities</u>

<u>Special Skills</u>

<u>Work Experience</u>

<u>Wardrobe</u>

Figure 2–4. Format for a résumé

(résumé size) sheet stating your name; social security number; telephone number(s); vital statistics, including age range and any infirmities (if you don't mind listing them) such as arthritis, dentures, glasses, hearing aid; your past profession; and any skills you might have.

Just show a great deal of enthusiasm. After all, we all have to start somewhere.

Other Items You'll Need

Before you can consider yourself a serious professional, you will also need picture postcards and a telephone service and/or answering machine.

Picture Postcards
Picture postcards are an excellent way of keeping in touch. Repeated mailings help to make your face familiar, and after a while agents almost think they know you. Postcards are also perfect for expressing your appreciation for interviews, auditions, and jobs. The front of this postcard will need your name and phone number, printed below your photograph. You can then write a message on the back, such as "Thank you"; "Look forward to working for you soon"; "Just did a shoot with Robert Redford"; etc. You may use the same photo you chose for your headshot, select your second choice, or use both. The photo reproduction house will show you several styles. (A photo reproduction house specializes in reproducing professional photographs for actors.) I suggest you check the ads in the trade publications or, better still, ask the photographer who takes your photo. It is in his interest to refer the best. You should have two hundred picture postcards printed, single or double photo (depending on the style you choose). Prices average around $70 for 50; $85 for 100; $130 for 200; and $250 for 500.

Telephone Services and/or Answering Machines
An answering device is sine qua non, an absolute essential. It is the performer's lifeline. After all, what good is all your effort

and talent if the agents and casting people can't reach you? Historically, "telephone services" have always been considered a vital part of an actor's package (the alternative is to sit by the phone and wait for it to ring). But times have changed. With the proliferation of voice mail and home answering machines, actors now have options.

Answering Services The traditional "answering service" is generally available in major cities throughout the country. The service provides you with a telephone number (which goes on your résumé) and a live operator to take your calls and messages. You may call as often as you deem necessary to check in for your messages (generally, a few times a day).

The cost for this service ranges from about $8.00 to $15.00 per month. In considering a service, it is most important that you choose one that is reputable and reliable and whose operators are pleasant, courteous, and take messages accurately. If you consider this option, you owe it to yourself to shop around for not only the best deal but also the most reliable results.

Voice Mail Then there's that recent addition, voice mail. This is very similar to the home answering machine, only it's the largest answering machine in the world. Subscribers use their own telephone numbers and record their own messages. They then can retrieve their messages anytime by simply punching in a preset number and security code. Voice mail subscriptions are generally much less expensive than the live answering service—but unlike the home answering machine, there is a monthly fee.

Home Answering Machines Another option is the home answering machine with a retrieval system, which allows you to call your machine when you are away. In my experience, and that of other actors I've spoken with, this has proven to be very convenient, efficient, and less costly, and it helps you to keep on top of things without missing opportunities.

Like the other services, you can call your machine from anywhere, seven days a week, twenty-four hours a day. (This is an added perk, especially when you are out of town.) Another advantage is that you can set your home phone to pick up your retrieval call on the first ring if you have messages. If there are no messages, the phone will ring three times before a charge is incurred. Because you can hang up on the second or third ring, you can avoid all charges and save lots of time and money.

A good machine can be purchased for less than $100. It is simple to install, requires very little maintenance, and has a long life. (I've had mine for more than eight years and it's still going strong.) This system has worked well for me. I've never missed a call or booking. I call my machine several times a day, and usually I can get back to the caller on the spot. And, of course, when I'm home, I can take my calls directly.

What the Agents Say Sylvia Fay, a New York casting director, likes both answering machines and services. She does advise actors with answering machines to keep their outgoing messages short. "The less said the better," she notes. She doesn't want to hear a barking dog or Beethoven's Fifth while she's waiting to leave her message. "Most important," Sylvia adds, "just make sure you call your machine or service often and get back to me as fast as you can."

Dorothy Palmer, a New York agent, prefers a telephone answering service. When she puts out a call, she can dial one number and leave messages for whoever subscribes to that service.

Grant Wilfley, another casting director, prefers answering machines. "It takes too long to give a service information," he says. Most others I've asked don't seem to have a preference. The most common word of advice was, "Just be easy to reach and respond quickly."

Record Keeping

I'm often asked, "Are my expenses deductible on my income tax?" They sure are. And that includes photos, résumés, telephone calls and systems, transportation, postal expenses, books, publications, courses, special clothing and makeup, etc. In other words, any legitimate business expense can be deducted.

To keep a record of your daily expenses, workday plan, mailings, and contacts, it is essential that you keep a diary. This can be a basic appointment book with enough room on each page to include your daily business activity (go-sees, auditions, interviews, rounds, mailings, etc.). And, of course, your future appointments and follow-up cards and calls should be recorded on the appropriate date.

Another important organizer is a business address book. (This could be in back of the diary or a separate item.) It should contain the names, addresses, and telephone numbers of agents, casting directors, professional services, union offices, other actors, schools, and programs available in your area.

Additionally, I've found it quite helpful to make notations in my book regarding the stage of the relationship I have with my contacts and any particulars I want to remember about the person or production. This information comes in mighty handy as you develop your business relationships. When you remember things about a person, it makes you kind of special. And that person, in turn, remembers you.

3

Modeling

Real People Are the Advertisers' Choice

Print Work

In the trade, the word *print* refers to the advertisements in printed publications such as magazines, newspapers, journals, and brochures. Commercial print work is modeling and posing for ads in the printed media.

I am often asked if print work is a part of show business. Most of the agents I talked to responded with an unequivocal yes. Print work is very much a part of the world of show business. You work in front of a camera, you portray a personality, and you are viewed by an audience. The process of creating ads for print and getting them to their final stages is quite similar to that of creating a television commercial (see Chapter 5). In fact, the same agencies are often involved in both.

Opportunities for Fifty-Plus

The word *modeling* usually evokes an image of high fashion, blue jeans, sex, and glamorous young models. Yet according to Paula Tackler of FunnyFace Today, a top modeling agency in New York City, the largest part of their business is with "real people," models who portray various types of characters—including upscale types and people of all ages. So the good news is that there is a healthy market for people of all sizes, shapes, types, and ages over fifty.

Paula agreed, as did the other agents I spoke with, that there is a good market for mature people. She added, "There is much work for the mature woman and man, but not as much as I expect there will be in the next five years."

Wally Rogers of R&L Model & Talent Management (another top New York agency) receives many calls for distinct personality types such as chairman of the board, mature doctor, Grandma, Grandpa, corporate head, and upscale retired person. "These," he says, "can only be filled by mature models." There is a large senior consumer market out there worth billions of dollars, and as the saying goes, "The ad that doesn't include the gray misses out on the green."

If you look through magazines—especially family ones and those publications like *Modern Age* that cater to mature readers—you will see many senior models. The same is true for organizational publications, financial and special-interest materials, etc. You will probably see an ad for a local bank depicting an entire family, including Grandma and Grandpa, or you may see an ad for a retirement community featuring a mature, healthy, happy couple. If you keep looking, you will see many ads that deal with products and industries using mature "real" people—professional models who more likely than not are in their second career.

The Pros and Cons of Modeling as a Second Career

Modeling as a second career is attractive to people from a wide variety of backgrounds. The pros include:

1. You can meet interesting people who are doing what you are doing.
2. The field is easier to enter than many other professions.
3. Formal credentials matter less than being at the right place at the right time.
4. The advertisers are looking for people of all ages and the market for fifty-plus is growing.
5. The monetary rewards can be substantial.

The cons include:

1. Modeling jobs are sporadic.
2. The field is highly competitive and the clients are just as particular when selecting older models as they are when selecting fashion and beauty models.
3. Traveling to and from the job might present a problem to some. If you live far from the location where ad agencies, agents, and photographers are, the hours you spend traveling might be a hindrance.

A word about traveling. Joan Lowry comes into New York City from Connecticut. She uses the ride productively. Joan tells me she writes her postcards, reads the trade publications, or sets up her schedule for her day in the city (which usually revolves around a go-see, an interview, making rounds, or a job). Sometimes she meets other actors on the bus or train, and they network and enjoy the ride together. However, Joe Gannon, an electrician who wanted to change his career for health reasons, found traveling a chore. He started the process (an appointment with me, photographers, agents), but what he didn't realize is that there is more time involved than the actual four-hour shoot. He then reevaluated his priorities.

Bea Delizio

Height: 5'5"
Size: 10
Eyes: Brown
Hair: Blonde
AFTRA
(212) 724-2800

Figure 3–1. Bea Delizio's print-work composite

The bottom line is that you do have to be "in town" at least several times a week, especially in the beginning. Then, when you're successful, you have to be there for the work as well. Besides the shoot, there are go-sees, rounds, interviews, networking, etc. How much you do and how busy you are is up to you, but the more involved you are, the more your chances of finding work are increased.

Modeling is really lots of fun. It's fun to work, it's fun to see yourself in the ads, and it's even more fun to get paid.

Tools and Preparation

Photographs

The first and most important step in modeling is to get a good photograph (see Chapter 2). Bear in mind that the agent's and client's first impression is almost always visual.

Photos are extremely important because the final form of most advertising work is the photo. The industry's standard for photos is to look real with as little retouching as possible (blemishes and heavy lines may be softened but not eliminated). Remember the golden rule: you must look like your picture. As you work, collect tear sheets or copies of the ads you appear in. Eventually, your agent will help you with a composite (three or four pictures in various poses, generally on a 5" x 7" card) and a portfolio.

Wally Rogers of R&L Model and Talent Management assured me that a headshot, at the beginning, is more than adequate. "If it doesn't work with a headshot, you certainly won't need a composite."

Gary Bertalovitz, an agent for McDonald/Richards, agrees. "Have a headshot that best represents you. Strong commercial style, middle America, big smile. Let your headshot work for you. Then collect tear sheets as you work to make a composite. Build a composite, not just a bunch of pictures."

Looking Good

Again, I repeat: your picture must look like you.

Hair Keep your hair neatly cut and styled like your picture. (You probably will have to get it cut a bit more often.)

Fingernails and Hands Your fingernails should be clean and neatly trimmed. Men should wear no nail polish or else wear natural nail polish. Women should wear natural, light, or none. You never know when your hands will be part of the shoot.

Makeup For women, makeup should be light and natural. For men, no makeup, except to cover blemishes or very dark circles. Max Factor (and I'm sure other cosmetic lines, too) sells a stick makeup called Erase, which is available at your drugstore or local makeup counter. It is available in shades to match your skin and is quite effective. It should be used lightly and blended in with surrounding skin areas.

Clothing A woman's closet should contain a business suit (no black or white), an upscale dress or dressy suit, a casual blouse, a sweater, pants, and a skirt. A man's closet should contain a dark business suit, a white shirt, simple-patterned tie, a casual open-collared shirt, a sweater, pants, a zippered jacket, a sport jacket, a flannel or cotton shirt, and dungarees. These outfits should be cleaned, pressed, hanging, and ready. You may get a quick call to model as a business executive, a grandpa, part of a couple on a cruise or vacationing, or perhaps one of two neighbors comparing their brands of fat-free sour cream. Always be ready—it's professional, and it's to your advantage.

Tips and Techniques

Facial Expressions
The model's face is responsible for selling the product. There is no voice or movement in a print ad, only facial expression.

Facial expression has to seem real. You don't want any expression that is so large it comes off as mugging, but you do want to exude personality and generate excitement. If you are feeling vacant, your eyes will reflect that vacancy. If you are

FRANK NUGENT   212-549-6971

Figure 3–2. Frank Nugent, in a dark business suit

thinking of nothing, your eyes will reflect emptiness. Have some motivation for whatever expression is on your face. Think about

- Eating a dish of your favorite ice cream (be specific).
- A reversal of bad news to good news.
- Someone you love coming to see you.
- Someone you hate coming to see you.

29

- Winning the lottery (be specific as to the amount and circumstances).
- Excruciating pain.

Build up a bank of personal experiences. Be very specific and use real incidents in your life. Practice them and be ready to use these expressions to show emotions of love, joy, pain, sadness, enthusiasm, pride, etc. If you think them, you will feel them. The expression will come from the gut, not just the lips or the eyes, and then it's real.

Dos and Don'ts for the Camera

Head The camera takes pictures in one dimension. If you bend your head forward too much, you will be emphasizing your forehead and your nose. A head bent too far backward will direct attention to the nostrils and chin and make you appear to be looking down your nose. Your head should be held in a natural way. Check this in a mirror. When you feel it and see it, you'll know it's right.

Hands Hands are often somewhat of a problem to beginning models. They seldom know where to put their hands, how to place them, or how to seem relaxed. If you are doing a sitting pose, put your hands gently in your lap. If standing, rest your wrists against your hips ever so lightly, just enough to give them support. Basically, your hands object to feeling like they're in midair. Practice different poses until you feel comfortable.

Cheating Cheating is a technique that is extremely important for you to know about, especially if you are working with other models or a product. In real life, you bend your head to read or to look directly at another model. For the camera, if you bend your head as much as you do normally, much of your face will be obscured from view. If you were to turn your head as you normally would to look at someone standing next to or slightly in back of you, all you would present to the camera would be your profile. In order to keep more of your face visible, you may be asked to "cheat," to look at one point while you appear to focus on another. To do this, turn your head at a forty-five-degree angle toward your partner. Then shift your eyes and focus them on a spot about five degrees more toward your partner. This way, you will be keeping your face angled more toward the camera so your audience can see it, yet by focusing on another point, you will appear to be looking directly at the other model. You will get the hang of it after a few tries.

Body If your head and hands look natural, your body will follow suit. Be sure your posture is straight but not stiff, and no slouching. Just keep it natural, comfortable, and in full view of the camera.

Working with Other Models If you are working with one or more other models, there are a few rules of etiquette. Be careful not to get in front or block him or her from view. If you are supposed to look as if you're leaning on another model, rest your arm or hand lightly. Most important, listen and follow the photographer's instruction. The photographer will place you in positions that will be best for the composition of the ad and for the product.

Personal Nutrition

It is very important that you keep your energy up. If you feel good, you'll look good. Most models I've talked with eat regularly. They make sure they have a balanced diet that includes lots of fruit, vegetables, fiber, and water.

Nella Griffin, an actress/model, has six small meals a day. She finds her energy lapses if she waits too long in between. The extra meals might just be a piece of fruit, a serving of yogurt, a cup of tea and a few crackers, or even a small glass of juice. This regimen keeps her energetic, looking good, and feeling great.

If you feel you would benefit from a more structured diet, I would suggest that you see a nutritionist. I'm sure your doctor can recommend one. There is also information available on nutrition in publications put out by the federal government.

The guidelines are excellent and the recommended food is nourishing and generally quite tasty.

Exercise

There are lots of ways to exercise: swimming, exercise class, dancing, walking, and bicycling are just a few suggestions. Even if your physical capacity is limited, do whatever you can that will help give you a sense of well-being. (Before you begin a program of diet and exercise, it is a good idea to see a doctor first. A thorough check-up will determine your course of action.)

Many people in the business agree that proper diet and exercise are more than just a means of maintaining your weight and providing energy. They reflect on the overall condition of your body, your skin, your hair, everything.

Bill Bowdren told me about a photographer who suggested that one of his clients (a model) go on a fat-free, sugar-free diet for one week, then come back for the photo session. The results were terrific. The look of the model greatly improved and he had a successful shoot. Bill is also a great believer in exercise. He notes, "Just keep moving, walking, dancing, even housework, just keep those muscles active. If you don't use it, you lose it."

Eat well, sleep well, take good care of yourself. As the saying goes, "Thorough preparation makes its own luck."

Modeling Agents

Do I Need an Agent?

Modeling agents are in the business to scout out new faces and act as a link between client and model. Agents

- Help you by reviewing and commenting on your photographs;
- Help you market yourself;
- Help you develop your portfolio and composite card;
- Negotiate rates, and,

- Most important, guide you to go-sees, which it is hoped lead you to jobs.

For print work you definitely need an agent. Modeling agencies are the first source clients turn to when they need models for their ads. The agent can supply numerous options to the client. Making one phone call to an agent can save the client lots of time and energy.

Should I Have More Than One Agent?
Absolutely. You should contact all agents, casting directors, and ad agencies. Your headshot and résumé should reach everyone who might be able to lead you to a booking.

See Appendix B for a current list of agents and casting directors for you to contact. While it is true that the majority of agents are in New York and Los Angeles, there are agents all over the country.

How to Spot a Disreputable Agent

1. Beware of money asked for up front. No legitimate agency takes an advance fee (regardless of whether it is a "registration" fee, or "consultation" fee, or any similar request).
2. Look askance at nonspecific ads in help-wanted columns in daily and Sunday newspapers, usually those stating "m/f no experience necessary."
3. Watch out if an agent pressures you to leave a deposit (usually cash) or pressures you to sign a contract immediately.
4. Be wary if the agent has a photography studio as part of his or her office and wants to sell you photograph sessions. (A legitimate agent should recommend two or three photographers at your request. The agent should not offer a direct service.)

Seeing the Agent
When you arrive for your appointment, bring at least eight or ten additional headshots and some picture postcards. If the agent is interested in you, he or she will want to send your headshot out to clients.

Be on time and dress comfortably and appropriately for your age, without heavy jewelry or tight clothes. Be friendly. Be confident. Remember, you offer your life experience and uniqueness. The agent's main interest in you is your headshot, but the agent will also expect you to be professional. It is necessary that you appear to be responsible, reliable, and enthusiastic.

Agents don't get bookings. They are there to get you contacts and appointments. However, you must provide the basis— your attitude, motivation, and, of course, your photo. An agency can work best for you if you work to maintain a relationship. Keep in contact by phoning or perhaps dropping by once a month.

The Agent's Commission
Normally a legitimate modeling agency takes a 20 percent commission from your wages after you have completed a job. Some agents pay the model shortly after the job is complete, but most wait until the client pays the agent. In either case, the agent's commission is deducted before the model is paid.

The average wage for a model is about two hundred and fifty dollars per hour, or it can be a day rate or a flat rate. Your agent generally takes care of the negotiations and tries to work out the best deal for you. I've done several jobs at a flat rate that paid between twelve hundred and fifteen hundred dollars. The jobs ran between three and four hours. Of course, that's not to say that the day could not have been longer.

Just recently, I booked a hand modeling job (they used only my hand holding a pill). The job paid the usual rate of two hundred and fifty dollars per hour. I worked two hours. A few days later I received a phone call telling me the film had gone bad and asking if I would be available for a reshoot. I was delighted to reschedule; I received another five hundred dollars. It all worked out fine. The client was happy, the photographer was happy, and I was certainly happy, especially when I received my double check. One point more: unfortunately there is no union governing print work. Hence models often don't get paid for as much as ninety days after the booking.

The Agency's Model Book

Most modeling agencies have a book depicting their stable of models. This book is sent out to their various clients. It is used as an additional marketing tool for the model and agent, and it works as a convenience for the client.

The charge to be part of the agency's book is anywhere from seventy-five dollars to two hundred and fifty dollars depending on the agency, how much space is devoted to each model, and how elaborate the book is. I would recommend that you go into the agency's book. When they send the books out to one thousand photographers, that's one thousand contacts being made for you.

A Final Word About Agents

What is all boils down to is this:

1. Choose an agency that appears to have work for your type.
2. Make sure they're reputable.

Most agencies know the kind of clients they do business with and can generally judge the type of models they represent.

The Go-See

It's always exciting to get a call from an agent sending you on a "go-see." The go-see is usually set up by the photographer to view models for the particular ad that is being planned. This usually takes place at the photographer's studio.

When the call comes in from the agent, I would suggest that you have a notepad and pen handy. Be sure to write

1. The location where the go-see will be held.
2. The time you are to be there.
3. What you should wear.

The Location

Make sure you understand exactly where the go-see is going to be. Get directions if you need to. Give yourself plenty of time to get there, and don't be late.

The Time

Go-sees are generally scheduled for a half day or possibly an entire day. For example, you will be told by your agent that the time is 9:00–1:00 or 2:00–5:00 or 10:00–4:00. You may get there any time during that period. However, the actual time it takes for you to be seen is usually only about five or ten minutes. The photographer will take a Polaroid of you and ask for your headshot. Sometimes the client may be there (very rarely in my experience). If so, he or she may want to interview you. The client is looking for confidence, enthusiasm, and a pleasant personality. Be honest, be natural, and be compliant

What You Should Wear

Wally Rogers of R&L Model & Talent suggests that you dress for the character as closely as you can. A perfect grandma, a politician, or an affluent retired person each demands a different costume. If your agent fails to give you an idea of what the character is like, ask. Always ask your agent if you're in doubt about the acceptability of a particular garment. When you are given a general suggestion of what to wear, relate it to specific clothing you own and ask the agent if your outfit will be appropriate for the call.

Knowing the Product/Client

It always helps to know the persona of the client: AT&T, Citicorp, MasterCard, General Foods, Pharmaceutical, etc. The more you know, the better prepared you can be—and the better the chances are for you to get the booking.

At the Studio

When you arrive at the photographer's studio, you will usually find a sign-in sheet that asks for your name, your agency, and the agency's phone number. Sign your name and fill in the above information. (Take a moment to glance at the other agency names. If some are not on your mailing list, add them.)

If you're like me, you've already been running around town, and you feel you need just a bit of a touch-up. After you fill out the sign-in sheet and before you have your picture taken, ask to see a mirror.

When you are ready, take out your headshot and wait your turn to have your picture taken. Use your time productively. Be observant. Pick up every cue. Pick up ideas from people who go before you. Watch what they do with their hands, how they stand, their facial expression. The photographer will give you directions, but a few creative ideas of your own never hurt.

After the photographer takes the Polaroid, you may be asked to wait a few minutes to make sure it came out. Then you are free for the rest of the day.

Accepting a Job

Typically you'll receive a phone call from your agent shortly after the go-see, asking if you are available for a shoot on a particular day. The agent will tell you who the client is, where the shoot is located, and what time you should be there. The agent should also tell you how much the hourly pay is and if there is a guaranteed number of hours. They should let you know when the wardrobe department will contact you and remind you to bring the tricopy voucher, which you'll need signed in order to be paid.

The Shoot

Let's think back to your photo session for your headshot. This gives you a good idea of what to expect. The job photo session will generally be about the same. However, there are some important differences:

1. Now you will be paid, instead of paying, to be photographed.
2. You will be expected to take directions and respond quickly. (This is where your bank of emotional experiences will come in handy.)
3. You will be under pressure that did not exist from your own photographer. This, at last, is the real thing!

Upon arrival make sure you check in (someone will be available to direct you). Come ten to fifteen minutes before call time, no earlier, no later. Display your wardrobe. The wardrobe people will then make the selection. If you were told not to wear makeup, come with your face clean. If you were told to come camera-ready, apply your makeup appropriately, look your best, and look like your headshot.

Makeup artists will more than likely be available for you and will put on the finishing touches. This will be true whether you are modeling as a homemaker making jam or as a midwestern farmer drinking a nonalcoholic beverage. The "look" they want will be created for you.

While you are getting ready, other professionals will also be preparing for the shoot. (There may be other models getting ready, or it may just be you.) Assistants will be setting up basic lighting and giving the set its final touches. The photographer is in charge and will be directing all this. The atmosphere may be charged with exhilaration, or there may be a feeling of anxiety in the air. It's your job to get ready quietly and quickly and wait for the shoot to begin.

Once the shoot begins, the photographer will give you directions. If you are to hold a product, you will be shown how to do so in order to minimize lighting glares and to prevent your fingers from covering the product's name.

When the shoot is finished, have the photographer or client fill out your voucher slip. Send it off to your agent as soon as possible. (The sooner the voucher gets to your agent, the sooner you get paid.) It is likely that you will not see a tear sheet or prints of the jobs you do. Depending on when and where the print is going to be used, you may never even see the final results. Or, your friends and family may spot the ad before you do!

Therefore, before you leave the studio, ask the photographer or the client when the tear sheets will be available and when you can call to obtain a copy. You will probably be told to get back to them in about a month or so. Make a note of whom to call, the number to call, and the date you are to call and be sure to follow up.

One model told me that she sends a self-addressed stamped envelope with a note saying that she was told the ad was ready and that she would appreciate a tear sheet for her portfolio. It worked for her. Whatever approach you use, the important thing is to get your copies so you can build your composite card and your portfolio.

You have done your first shoot. Be sure to mail or deliver your voucher to your agent. And now you are ready for your next go-see.

4

Extra Work
The Corps de Ballet of Show Business

In *Webster's Dictionary*, the word *extra* is defined as "something additional," like an additional point or score, or the icing on a cake. An "extra" on television and in the movies is the added ingredient that not only enhances the production but also lends a sense of reality to the work and makes it believable.

Grant Wilfley, a New York City casting director for Wilfley Todd, describes an extra as "an actor who does nonspeaking roles." He stresses the importance of extras in films and cites the following examples of extras in a courtroom scene:

- The jury.
- The spectators.
- The Assistant D.A.
- The guards.
- Any other people in the scene who do not have a speaking role.

He also draws attention to the oddness of a street scene without people: "Movies are generally about people; you must have people to have a film."

Just imagine a scene with Robert Redford and Barbra Streisand in a New York City subway car during rush hour, with not a soul in sight—just the two of them alone. Eerie isn't it? And certainly not natural. The scene should be bustling with people: passengers, beggars, conductors, and people on the platform all contribute to the reality of the scene.

It works the same in television. For example, in one episode of *Seinfeld*, Jerry and Elaine, two of the principles, were in a movie theater. The extras in the scene (the rest of the audience) were

40

reacting to the movie. Their reactions made us, the television audience, understand the movie Jerry and Elaine were watching and served to create a very real audience/movie situation.

Extras also lend to the atmosphere, mood, and time period of a film. For example, they serve to distinguish different types of restaurants (highbrow, ethnic, neighborhood); boats (cruise, immigrant, tourist, transport, pirate ship); neighborhoods (upper class, middle American, urban, suburban, European, Asian); sects (Mormon, Amish, Quaker); eras (Roman, Victorian, historical, biblical, modern); etc. Extras help to transplant viewers in time and place and further enhance their enjoyment of the film.

A Bit About Extras

Where Do Extras Work?

Extras work in movies, soaps, television commercials, print ads, and theaters. Even the opera uses extras (here they are called supernumeraries). Extras represent all types of people, in all walks of life, in all time periods.

When I worked as an extra on *Billy Bathgate* (there were many of us over fifty), my role was a society lady in the Roaring Twenties. I was impressed by the attention given to every detail of my clothing, makeup, and hair—from the tips of my shoes to the top of my hat—including seamed stockings, jewelry, handbag, and gloves of that era. When they had me "camera ready," I hardly recognized myself. I truly felt transported in time.

Extras go to weddings and funerals, eat in restaurants, shop in stores, stroll in the park, walk on the street, work in hospitals, and so on. They are patients, shoppers, salespeople, police officers, hotel staff, the homeless. They ride the subways, take buses, drive cars, go to parties, do crowd scenes, and a lot more. They do the same things you do in real life.

Is There Work for Seniors?

Mature extras are working all the time. People are living longer and staying healthy, and the film industry reflects the population. Casting directors are open to new people of all ages, and seniors are a very significant part of the "casting call."

You should note that there is competition, and the hours are irregular (you can work from sunup to sundown on one job or two to three hours on another—each for a "day's" pay). Furthermore, once you make a commitment to work, you must be reliable (you are generally advised at the time of the booking as to the number of days involved).

Nonetheless, doing extra work is excellent on-the-job training. It is an opportunity to meet and work with notables in the business and a chance to observe actors and directors and learn how to work in front of a camera by doing. It provides you with the experience of working on the set and, more important, an opportunity to be seen.

This could be a splendid beginning of a career. If it appeals to you and you're game to try, let me show you how to apply your life experience, how to make contacts, and how to use your newly gained knowledge.

Can I Go Beyond a Nonspeaking Role?

That depends on you and on luck. There are possibilities. The most important factor is that you have to be there. You have to be where the action is: on the set, in the studio, on location. There are character roles (more for men than for women) that may call for just your type.

In other words, extra work offers the additional opportunity of being upgraded on the set. It is possible to be promoted to a speaking part (which can be one word or five pages of dialogue).

Frank Nugent, a retired sales manager, has done more than twenty-five extra jobs in the course of several years. He told me that he has had several upgrades. In *84 Charing Cross Road*, starring Anne Bancroft and Anthony Hopkins, Frank was upgraded to a newsvendor, with one line. Because of this, his name appeared on screen in the cast of characters at the film's conclusion. In addition, he received a considerable increase in pay (from $99 to $485 base pay for the day).

Frank talks glowingly about working in a dance scene with Anne Meara. He has also worked closely with Shelley Long, Judith Ivey, and Cliff Gorman, to name a few. In addition, he worked with Lou Jacobi, and they've been good friends ever since.

The opportunity for upgrades comes in many ways. Another extra, who was hired as a mourner in a funeral scene, was upgraded to a funeral director (a small speaking part). He was chosen because he was wearing a dark suit. The original actor who was to play the part apparently misunderstood the clothing assignment (it's so important to get the instructions correct).

Joe K., an extra playing one of several kitchen helpers in a television pilot, was upgraded to cook. This occurred because there was a script change, and Joe evidently looked the part. He enjoyed the experience, had a good addition for his résumé (which probably got him more work), and welcomed the added money.

I also have had several experiences being upgraded. My first time was on the soap *One Life to Live*. I was hired as an extra on a train and was upgraded to a newspaper reporter, which was a small speaking part. This led to getting my Screen Actor's Guild card (see Chapter 9) as well as a sizable increase in pay.

As you get known, you usually can be an extra more often. Extra work can be your main focus, or it can serve to fill in the gap between your other jobs in print and television commercials. It keeps you involved and busy, provides the opportunity for making new contacts, and adds to your income. For those of us who want the atmosphere of show business (extra work, print work, and possibly commercials), it certainly is an appealing way to be part of the glamour and enjoy a second career.

Preparation for the Job

Generally, agents do not get paid for getting actors extra work. Therefore, it is up to you to make the contacts and keep abreast of the casting notices.

Before you begin, you need the following:

- An 8" x 10" headshot and résumé;
- A list of casting directors (see Appendix B);
- A cover letter (brief, to the point, and polite);
- Clothing that is clean, pressed, and ready to wear;
- Picture postcards for follow-up and for future contacts;
- An answering machine and/or service; and
- You—"camera-ready."

Making the Initial Contact

Send out your 8" x 10" photo to your list of casting directors. Be sure to attach your résumé to your photo, and enclose a cover letter, which should say something to the effect of "I'm available for extra work." It should also include union affiliation, indicating that you are nonunion if this is the case. (Do not hesitate to say *nonunion*. The casting directors use a large number of nonunion people, and they need this information for casting.) Also make sure your name and telephone number are clear and accurate.

About seven working days later, follow this mailing with another mailing using your picture postcard. Say something like "Just keeping in touch" or "Looking forward to your call." Be sure to mention any relevant experience you've had since your first mailing.

Generally a headshot should be sent to your mailing list every three to six months.

You don't have to contact the entire list at once. A system I find that works quite well is to send five headshots and résumés each day, following up with five picture postcards seven days later, until I've worked my way through the list. In the meantime, there may be additions to your mailing list, such as notices you will come across in the trade papers and publications, as well as contacts you make through networking.

It is very important for you to keep accurate records (dates, names, telephone numbers) of all contacts you make, mailings, follow-ups, people you meet, and people who send you out. Also be sure to exchange names, addresses, and telephone numbers with people with whom you work. There's a lot of networking in the business. Remember, today's extra may be tomorrow's star.

Sending Additional Picture Postcards

Most casting directors suggest that after the first two contacts are made, you send picture postcards about once a month. Some say more often. However, here's a little hint: while the film is in production, send the casting director a picture post-card weekly. There are times in the course of filming when the casting director may call for additional actors because of scene changes, script changes, actor availability, etc. Sending your photo while they are shooting will provide additional opportunities for you to be considered for the job.

Finding Out When They Are Casting

Check the trade papers and publications for announcements of open calls and other casting notices. Also watch for announcements of new movies. There will generally be some information about the film that can be helpful when you make your contact.

When they were shooting *State of Grace*, with Sean Penn, I had read that it dealt with many Irish Americans. I immediately sent a note to the casting director with my headshot saying, "My friends tell me I have a face like the map of Ireland. I'd be good for your film." The call came a few days later, and I worked on the shoot for a week.

The more information you have about a film or a soap, the more professional you can be. For example, when you send your picture and cover letter to the casting people, you might suggest a part for yourself as I did for the film *State of Grace*. If you are called for an interview (there are times when a casting director will interview actors for extra work for particular scenes and for bit parts), being knowledgeable will help you feel more comfortable. It also allows you to bring more depth and understanding to the interview.

When casting directors put ads for extras in the trade or local papers, they are quite specific about their requirements. They generally specify age range, types, special clothes, special talents (ballroom dancer, car driver, etc.). The ad might even include particular scenes such as weddings, funerals, and parties. This information provides the actor with the opportunity to bring appropriate clothes and props to the audition or open call. The ad will also specify union or nonunion.

When nonunion is listed, follow their instructions and go at the given time. Bring your headshot and résumé and dress appropriately. If they do not call for nonunion, do not go. (They check union cards before they allow you in.) However, in that case I would suggest that you mail your headshot to the casting director with a note stating your nonunion status and that you'd like to be considered for extra work.

Other casting directors may hold an open call or specify "open access," which is an invitation for actors to visit their offices at specific times. Most stipulate that they do not want phone calls. (They are busy people, and having calls coming in would disrupt the casting calls they have to make.) As Sylvia Fay says, "Keep in there, but don't call me, I'll call you."

A Checklist

1. Mail your 8" x 10" headshot, résumé, and cover letter to everyone on your list.
2. Follow up with your picture postcard seven working days after your initial contact.
3. Follow up with your picture postcard once a month, but more often when you know a casting director has a film in production.
4. Read the trade papers and publications and network. (As Sarah Hyde Hamilton, a New York casting director says, "You've got to know the business of show business.")

Getting the Phone Call

The phone call will usually come after you've done your mailing and made your contact and the casting director has a film in production. With soaps, casting directors will generally call you for an interview (they like to see you in the flesh); however, some will book you right from your headshot.

When the phone rings, the conversation will go something like this: "Hi, this is Laura from Sylvia Fay's office. Are you available for extra work on Tuesday?" Your answer should be an enthusiastic yes. Laura will then proceed to give you the date(s), day(s), time, place, and most important, information about how to dress (color and type of clothing). Be brief, be pleasant, be polite. Get the caller's name and the name of the casting director for your files.

The Day of the Shoot

Dress in the outfit you discussed previously with the person from wardrobe or the casting director. Be sure to come in the colors you agreed on. That's quite important because they are looking at the scene as a whole, and there might be different colors for different extras. Take an additional top or outfit, just to give them a choice.

The meeting place may be the location of the shoot or it may be that you are meeting a bus to go elsewhere. The bus will take you and the other extras to another part of town, a nearby town, a suburb, or even an airport (in *Scent of a Woman*, we were taken to Newark Airport).

When you arrive at the designated location, the person in charge will direct you to the holding area. There will usually be a table of coffee, tea, bagels, and lots of delicious goodies. There will be a bathroom available, and a telephone within a reasonable distance. Here are some key points you'll need to remember:

- It is very important that you stay in the holding area until you are called to the set. If you have to go to the bathroom or make a telephone call, let the person in charge know where you are.
- Know the name of the person in charge.
- Make sure you've been seen by wardrobe and your clothes have been approved. (If you've brought an extra change, this is the time to show it.)
- When you are called to the set, be camera-ready (clothing, hair, makeup, etc.); don't go off to primp.

The person in charge will guide you to where you should be. Follow directions, listen carefully, do not look at the camera, be at the right place at the right time, and be pleasant and cooperative.

I asked several casting directors, What are the requisites for being an "extra" good extra? They all agreed on the following points:

1. Be on time.
2. Listen carefully and follow directions.
3. Be aware; don't get in the way.
4. Be professional.
5. Have a nice pleasant attitude.
6. Enjoy the shoot.

After the Shoot

Congratulations, you've had your first shoot. If you followed the guidelines, I'm sure it went well and you were an "extra" good extra.

Keeping the Contact

Most important, be sure to send the casting director who hired you your picture postcard with a note to the effect of, "Thanks for the shoot; it was great working for you" or "Thanks for thinking of me; I look forward to working for you again soon." Make sure your note is brief, polite, and to the point. It's also a good idea to send out some cards to the people you've worked with, such as the director, assistant director, etc. The content of this message could be something like, "I enjoyed meeting you and look forward to working with you again." It never hurts to be courteous.

At this point—you guessed it—send postcards to the rest of your mailing list to tell them you've worked on a film. Actually, anytime you have something to say pertinent to your work (a shoot, a unique outfit or uniform you might have acquired, an acting course you might be taking, a change of address, or just another hi to keep in touch), it's a good idea to communicate it to your mailing list.

Here's a checklist for keeping the contact: to get more work

1. Keep up with your mailings.
2. Keep accurate and good records.
3. Read the trade papers and publications.
4. Be aware—keep your ears open and network with your fellow actors.

You will find that many of your fellow actors who do print and extra work expand their horizons by entering the world of commercials. So read the next chapter and follow the yellow brick road.

5

Commercials

Mature Products Need Mature People

Acting in commercials is a specialized field demanding unique skills, concentration, and techniques. But once you get started, it can prove to be a lucrative part of your career.

Although most commercials are union, you don't have to be a union member to work. Many nonunion commercials are being shot in almost all sections of the country, including the big cities. The major difference between union and nonunion is the payment of residuals (most union actors receive payment every time their commercial is shown).

Paying particular attention to this chapter—understanding how a commercial becomes a reality, examining skills and techniques, and discovering what occurs in the audition room—will help you determine, Are commercials for me? Here are a few facts:

1. Ninety-eight percent of all American households have television sets.
2. The average household has its set turned on for six hours and forty-five minutes a day, every day of the year.
3. Seven minutes of every hour is devoted to selling something.
4. The reason most of us buy one product rather than another is because of a television ad.

The commercial creates an image to seduce the public, and the television industry's primary source of income is the sale of airtime to advertisers. According to one recent survey, advertisers spend over thirteen billion dollars each year to broadcast their commercials. Television commercials are big business, with big money. Consequently, a vast number of commercials are shot, which increases your employment opportunities.

The Development of a Commercial

The advertising agency is hired by the client to promote sales. The account executive at the ad agency and the marketing executives for the client decide who their target group will be (age, socioeconomic status, sex, etc.) and how they can best approach them. After this decision is made, a copywriter creates specific commercials for approval. These are then presented to the client. When the client is satisfied, the commercial is ready to roll.

At this point, a production company is hired to film the commercial. The production company and ad agency staff begin working together to finalize all details (location, casting, and so forth). Many of the large agencies have their own casting departments. Otherwise, separate agencies are employed to do the casting. At any rate, casting people then hold auditions.

Finally, the actors are selected. At this point, the commercial is ready to be produced. The cast, the creative team, and the production people assemble on the shooting day.

After the commercial is shot, it goes to the film editor. After the editing process, the commercial is ready to be viewed by the public.

Shooting Commercials

There are similarities in shooting a commercial and doing print work. The emphasis here is still strongly on the visual, with careful attention given to makeup, hair, and wardrobe. You will still be playing a role in front of the camera, on a set, with the same lighting setups. There will be numerous takes filmed to achieve the desired result. Now, however, additional skills will be called for. You must be able to move easily, appear relaxed, memorize lines, and deliver those lines in a natural way.

Who Gets the Jobs?

Years ago it was considered wise to choose only the young and the beautiful to appear in commercials. Casting directors looked for the prettiest people they could find to capture the public's attention.

But the ad agencies soon learned that the average viewer had difficulty in identifying with the glamorous performer. A typical grandmother would remark, "I just can't believe that beautiful model is cleaning her daughter's stove." Yes, the perfect starlet still sells the hair products, the cosmetics, and the perfumes, and the young handsome males sell men's grooming products, but many other products are sold by people who could be your next-door neighbor—people with whom the viewer can identify.

Do I Qualify?

This is one of the most frequently asked questions. If you watch television commercials, you will discover that the answer is probably yes. Commercials use many different types of actors because consumers are different.

What Are the Opportunities?

An actor may have a "look" that will be just what the casting director is looking for. Take Minnie Horowitz, a retired accountant who never took an acting course in her life. Seven years ago she booked the first commercial she ever auditioned for when her friend and manager Betty Geffen thought she had the right look. Since then she's worked regularly in TV and print. Minnie has done spots for Con Edison, Hebrew National, Parker Brothers, Miller Beer, Chuka Cheese, Sonic Fast Food, and Steve's Gourmet Ice Cream and at age ninety-five is currently appearing in a Humana commercial.

Minnie is very excited about her life and career. "I just love this work, it makes me happy, and I can't help sharing my happiness with others." She is totally surprised to find herself in the acting profession. "Who would have thought I would be doing this work at this time in my life." Then Minnie adds, "I'm having a great time and I look forward to every job."

While there are some actors who make a terrific living exclusively from doing commercials, the majority find the business difficult. It's tough and highly competitive, and its even tougher for "mature" folks. According to *Back Stage*, the biggest age-group for casting is twenty-eight- to thirty-five-year-old men and women because this is the population that has the greatest disposable income and starts having families. Children and teens are runners-up. Casting slows down around college age because that age-group spends less. However, the good news is that the advertisers are beginning to recognize that the fifty-plus population does have the money to spend, especially on the products and services pertinent to their life-style.

Bob Colliers, an actor and head of a commercial school, has been heard to say that he gets more auditions now that he's over fifty than ever before. Actress Carole Lavin, whom you met in Chapter 1, enthusiastically says, "I feel I've reached a good age for commercials. I fit into a good niche."

Another piece of good news is that the trend seems to be for vignette-style commercials composed of quick scenes using different actors. This involves larger casts. A New York casting director noticed that eight years ago, every vignette commercial had a minimum of fifteen characters. Then it dropped to one or two. But now larger casts with eight or ten characters are slowly coming back. These almost always include one or two fifty-plus actors.

Preparation, Tips, and Techniques

A must for every person who intends to work in commercials is to watch television commercials. One of the best ways you can research the field is to study the spots you see. Here is a partial list of the more common types used in commercials for fifty-pluses.

The granny
The spokesperson
The senior executive
The patient
The father
The granddad
The retired couple
The police captain
The doctor
The head nurse
The judge
The teacher (the one "who changed my life")

Choose a few you feel comfortable with, and closely observe their clothing, hairstyle, facial expressions, and voice. Repeat their words right after them. Try to make the lines sound as real and convincing as you can.

Another exercise to sharpen your technique is to observe people. For example, shy people and outgoing people do not have the same mannerisms. They walk differently. Their expressions of emotions such as happiness, sadness, anger, and fear will be varied. Notice and learn as much as you can.

Now to the more specific techniques for doing the job.

Analyzing the Script

Commercials are written to introduce and sell merchandise. Your job is to discover the essence, the basic core of the commercial, and project it. Therefore it is most important to understand what you are saying. Appendix A provides samples of commercial copy. With each piece of copy, ask yourself, What makes this product different or better than other similar products? If it is not obvious, look for words or phrases in the copy that are repeated.

Ask yourself more specific questions, and try to find the answers in the copy. What kind of product is it? What is its name? What is it for? How much does it cost? Examine the script fully. Understand the overall purpose or message and the meaning of each sentence as it fits into the purpose. Let's take the sentence, "Aspirin's never been this easy to take." It sounds like a simple enough sentence with a direct meaning. However, if you change the emphasis from one word to another, the sentence takes on a new meaning. For example, "*Aspirin's* never been this easy to take." This means that unlike aspirin, the new product is easy to take. Try "Aspirin's *never* been this easy to take." This means that never in a million years has aspirin been this easy to take. Or "Aspirin's never been this *easy* to take." This means it's so easy to take this aspirin.

Reading

Practice saying thoughts rather than reading words. Read copy from magazine and newspaper ads into a tape recorder and listen to yourself. Use inflections in your voice and try not to sound flat. The way to become more proficient at reading aloud is to practice reading aloud.

If you are going to emphasize certain thoughts or words in the copy, don't hit the small connecting words like *but, and, so,* and *if.* Emphasize descriptive words. If you are performing in a pharmaceutical-related commercial, emphasize words like *relief, remedy, comfort, aid, ease, help.* If you are working in a food-related one, emphasize words like *yummy, delicious, crunchy, juicy,* and *luscious.*

For your purposes, reading aloud for about fifteen minutes a day should help develop good reading skills. Read anything you can get your hands on— a brochure, a flyer, or even a book you are currently reading.

When you are comfortable with your reading, it's time to add eye contact. The objective is to look your listener in the eye as much as possible while you are reading. Practice by using something that won't distract you. I found that securing a black spot (a round piece of black paper about three inches in diameter) to an empty wall with cellophane tape served my purpose well. Scan each sentence as you read, and try to look at the wall every few sentences. This might seem difficult at first, but it won't take long to get the hang of it.

Think of the spot as the camera eye. As you work with it, it becomes more comfortable and friendly. Picture someone real and specific that you are talking to (your child, your spouse, your grandchild, your best friend). The trick is to make the copy sound like it's written in your own words.

Coloring Words

Another technique for varying your delivery is to "color" the words. In particular, look for adjectives in every script. You want to make a word sound like what it says, just as you "color" words when you speak in everyday conversation. For example, you say "fabulously wonderful," "it's marvelous," "unheard of," "knock 'em dead," "oh boy," "fantastic," and so on. You make these words sound exciting. We express emotion more freely in everyday conversation than we do when we are reading. Try to include that emotion as you read.

Note, however, that even though you should have high energy while saying the dialogue, you shouldn't rush the copy. Actors tend to get nervous and run through the copy entirely too rapidly. We must give our audience time to let the message sink in.

Making Transitions

Attitude changes are the key points in commercials. Our voice and attitude automatically change when we move from one thought to the next. Look at the following dialogue.

Person A: My sauce is always sooo bland . . .
Person B: Try Ragu.
Person A: This is delicious; no more bland sauce in my house!

You can see the change in attitude (transition) from "My sauce is always sooo bland" to "No more bland sauce in my house!" Such transitions can be from negative to positive, dismayed to pleased, unconcerned to aware.

Transitional points usually occur when the solution is presented and when the problem is resolved. Make sure your attitude changes accordingly.

Projecting

When you are working on camera, there is no need to project your voice very loudly because the microphone is generally near you. Talk as you would to a friend sitting next to you at a party, or, if your scene partner is a camera three feet away, follow your natural impulse to project that far. This is not to say that your energy level should be low. Quite the contrary. Many commercials are bigger than life and demand much more energy than would a similar real-life situation. The animation should be visible in your face. Use your bank of personal experiences (see Chapter 3) as needed. The usual rule of thumb in commercial acting is to make it big. The director can always pull you down.

Categorizing Commercials

Commercials come in various forms, calculated to enchant the consumer. Here are some of them.

Spokesperson

The spokesperson is someone who is talking directly into the camera to sell a certain product. He or she talks to the audience one-to-one, trying to convince the consumer. The spokesperson always speaks with authority.

To practice working as a spokesperson, examine your favorite product that you use at home, a product you feel works for you (a specific brand of hemorrhoidal suppositories, cleaning tablets for false teeth, stain remover, raisin bran cereal, furniture polish, etc.). Analyze why this particular item is better than the rest: why you like it so much and what it does for you. It may be the secret of the year that you're willing to share with your best friend. Create your own commercial. Use your tape recorder to catch your enthusiasm and sincerity.

Slice-of-Life Commercials

These consist of a short story that usually contains a beginning, a middle, and an end. In this type of commercial, it is as though the camera were eavesdropping for a few moments into some people's lives. There is a problem presented ("My head is aching"), a possible solution ("Try Bayer aspirin"), and a resolution ("Thanks Bayer, the party's on"). This type of commercial has everyone living happily ever after. In my example, the aspirin completely solves their problems, and their lives are altered for the better.

Unlike a spokesperson, the actors in slice-of-life commercials relate to each other and never look into the camera unless the script says to do so.

Practice working in a slice-of-life commercial by visualizing yourself in the story. Who are you talking to? Be very specific. Establish a relationship with your partner by creating real characters. Make it sound believable. Don't keep looking at your scene partner. Keep actively glancing, listening, and doing. The scene should always be realistic. Make a definite statement ("Thanks Bayer, the party's on"). Let your audience know how grateful you are because your partner suggested Bayer.

The Vignette

This is a commercial composed of quick scenes using different actors. Each actor does something (usually looking into the camera) with energy and enthusiasm. It could be saying the name of the product, describing the product, or even having a silent reaction to the product.

To practice the vignette, live the moment, because behavior is based on cause and effect and the ability to appear believable even with no words, one word, or a sentence. For example, "Ummm, this soup is delicious." Replicate the taste, concentrate on how it would feel inside your mouth, then express that experience.

Now that we've covered some of the major commercial styles, let's proceed to the audition. Remember, auditions are obtained via agents, casting directors, and trade publications (see Chapter 7).

The Audition

When you arrive, one half hour before call time, you enter the waiting room and sign in (sign-in sheets are usually like those

58

at the go-see). Pick up the copy (if there is any) and check the storyboard (a large sheet of cardboard with a series of drawings depicting the different scenes in a commercial), which is usually taped to a wall. Go someplace private (restroom, down the hall) and analyze your copy, understand it, sell yourself on the product, and memorize the first and last lines.

The Audition Room

When you are called in, greet the casting director and the others in the room with a smile and a cheery hello. Introduce yourself, shake hands, and give your picture/résumé to whoever seems in charge.

Once you are in position to begin the audition, you will be asked to slate (to identify yourself on tape). Your slate is your vocal calling card, so it should not be done casually. It is the beginning of your performance and should be delivered with the same care as any line in your script. Wait until the cameraperson gives you the signal to start by saying action or just nodding in your direction. Look directly into the lens and smile, and with all the assurance in the world say, "Hi, my name is Nellie Newstar." Pause after your slate.

You will probably be using cue cards or hand-held scripts. It is most important that the camera gets a clear view of your face. Always angle your face toward the camera so both of your eyes can be seen. If your are holding your script, hold it low enough so it isn't in view of the camera and high enough so that the camera sees your entire face, not the top of your head. Don't hold it to one side, either. Practice at home in front of a mirror. See how you do.

More Tips About the Audition

You should approach an audition enthusiastically. Believability and enthusiasm are the two major factors in getting a job.

Be sure to listen to whatever the person in charge has to say. Assume that if any additional instructions are given to you, they are extremely important. If you don't understand something in the copy or a verbal instruction, make sure you ask before the audition begins. If you don't know a pronunciation or the meaning of a word, ask.

If you immediately fluff the first line, stop. It probably won't be a disaster; just start over. When you're a few lines into the script and you mess up a line, just act like nothing happened and continue. This shows you have composure and won't fall apart during the actual shooting. Continue to the conclusion, and then say, "May I try again?" or "Let me get the words straight and do it again."

Start the reading with a bang by delivering that first line while looking directly into the camera. Finish the same way. It can mean a booking.

Don't die out on the rest of the copy. There's always a tendency to lose energy about halfway through the script. Take your time, and make the words count.

How Will I Know If I Got the Job?

If you're cast in the commercial, you'll be notified through your agent. Keep in mind that if you're not cast, that doesn't necessarily mean that whoever was in charge didn't like you or your acting. You simply might not be the best type for the job, or they might have been "matching" people for the commercial. For instance, let's say the casting people were looking for a family who looked like they came from the heartland. But suppose you look like a city career type. Obviously you wouldn't be what they were looking for physically (they may have wanted to see several types before they made a decision). It wouldn't matter how terrific your reading was; you probably wouldn't have gotten the part. Also remember that there were many people seen for that commercial, so the odds were high. But don't be discouraged. Think of each audition as a learning experience in preparation for future opportunities.

In this business, rejection is a major part of the game. The odds are that if you stick with it, you will increase the probability of acceptance, and sooner or later you may be right for the part.

Money

How Are Actors in Commercials Paid?

For guidelines, let's start with union scale. The initial payment for the shoot, or *session*, is $443.25 for up to eight hours. Nine to ten hours equals time and a half. More than ten hours pays double time. You get recompensed with a fee equal to the first session every thirteen weeks, for a maximum period of twenty-one months, after which the contract is renegotiated. In addition, every time the commercial airs, you receive residuals, which vary with the category of the commercial (local, regional, national). The best-paid commercial is one that will run nationally as many times a day for as many days as possible.

Another common practice used for payment is a *buy-out*. This is an arrangement whereby the producer, actor, and agent agree on a flat fee for the twenty-one-month period. I did a buy-out for the United Way that totaled one thousand dollars over a period of several cycles.

Television commercial extras are paid $240 for up to an eight-hour day; time and a half for eight to ten hours; and double time after that.

A nonunion actor in a commercial is generally paid one fee for the day of the shoot. Bea Delizio, whom you met in Chapter 3, recently did a commercial that paid her five hundred dollars. Bill Bowdren's last commercial paid him six hundred dollars for three hours' work. Malcolm Beers has earned up to five hundred dollars per commercial. Most nonunion actors I've talked with make anywhere from two hundred to six hundred dollars for a day's shoot.

How Much Can I Earn?

Actresses like Patti Karr, age sixty-two, whose major thrust is television commercials, find they come in "bunches." Recently Patti did several commercials back-to-back—and then nothing. As she says, "That's the business."

Carole Lavin found that after eight months of rounds and mailings, she landed a national commercial. During her first year in show business, Carole was on unemployment. Three days after she received her last unemployment check, her first residual arrived. Now into her second year, Carole has earned about twenty-five thousand dollars and is very encouraged. Florence McGee, the ninety-two-year-old actress I mentioned in Chapter 1, has done a plethora of commercials. When I asked her about money, she said, "I don't know exactly how much I've made [and still make], but I've been living well, invested wisely, and have enough for my old age."

Do I Need Other Income?

Unfortunately, creative arts like writing and acting do not pay the average practitioner astronomical dividends. There are those who hit it and do very well; there are the experienced actors who practice their craft and earn a modest living; and, of course, there are those who, while enamored with their craft, show little in the way of financial remuneration.

6

Agents and Casting Directors

The Inside Scoop

Agents are businesspeople trying to make a living like most other professionals. Their function is locating people for their clients. Other facets of their job include securing auditions and go-sees and negotiating contracts and money for the actor/model. Even though the agents do not actually get you the job, they do put you in the right place at the right time. For this service, agents generally receive 10 percent of the pay you receive for on-camera work and 20 percent for print work.

There are many myths about agents. Some associate the word *agent* with "star" agencies like William Morris and International Creative Management (ICM), or they think of an agent as "too busy" and/or unattainable.

Yes, some agents may be "too busy," and a few may only talk to stars. However, there are hundreds of agents in the commercial and print field who will see you as marketable and be eager to represent you.

Casting directors, on the other hand, play a different role in the actor's life. Although casting directors generally depend on the agents to locate and recommend actors, they do, on occasion, call people directly.

Casting directors usually contact actors directly to work as extras. Sometimes when asked to fill other roles, they will call the "right person" from their headshot files and/or from personal contact. Casting directors do not receive a commission. Therefore, what you earn is all yours.

In talking with many agents and casting directors, I found that most agree on the qualities they look for in an actor: enthusiasm, energy, reliability, and professionalism.

A Closer Look

The roles of the agent and the casting director are all too frequently looked on as arcane and mysterious. It may provide an entree into the minds of agents and casting directors by having them explain what they do and what they look for.

Agencies

Central Casting of Florida
10 NE 11th Avenue
Ft. Lauderdale, FL 33301
(305) 525-8351
Central Casting is strong on mature actors. The agency is well known for its creative force in the industry. Its calls are mostly for commercials and television, but it does include extra and print work.

Thirty-eight years ago, Marian Polan of Central Casting established the first commercial all-film agency in Florida. Previously, her bookings had been mostly for nightclub acts and entertainment. Then she had an epiphany.

In the late 1950s, Marian realized that Florida's climate has a unique feature. The sun rises early and sets late most of the year. Armed with this "fact," she proceeded to New York City to canvas advertising agencies, production companies, etc. Her first words to them were, "How would you like to save sixty thousand dollars?" She explained how the long hours of sunlight would enable them to shoot two commercials in one day and/or film outdoors from 6:00 in the morning to 7:00 or 8:00 at night. This approach brought her many clients, and the rest is history. Her sharp observation of Florida's sun led to a flourishing market for commercial actors and models.

The agency is still very active, and daughter Enid Polan Howell is at the helm. Marian, at eighty years of age, is still a vital force, although semiretired. The agency's actors are both union and nonunion. Marian notes, "People have been with the agency since its inception. Some of them are in their seventies and eighties, and we're always looking for more."

The agency doesn't like to use the word *model* for commercials, print, and television. Its clients are "image makers," the actors who best represent the people they portray.

Marian's actors have been cast for a plethora of television commercials, commercial print, and over-forty movies. The agency has a special department for ethnic talent, specializing in Latinos.

When I questioned her about income, Marian said, "Earnings can depend on whether the actor is union or nonunion. Union wages can be anywhere from several thousand to a hundred thousand depending on how often the commercial is shown. Nonunion commercials have a wide range of payment. Wages depend on ads shot for local, national, or world consumption."

Marion is always in the market for retired people available for work (filming is usually in the daytime). She says, "Send in your picture. It could be any kind, as long as it looks like you."

FunnyFace Today
151 East 31st Street
New York, NY 10016
(212) 686-4343
In addition to representing upscale and "real" people, including children, characters, and people with disabilities, FunnyFace Today has added a new division called Products Promotion. This department uses actor/models of all ages to work in department stores, malls, and other locations, to interact with people to promote a product. This new division is one more venue for advertisers to sell their product and provides more opportunity for jobs.

Many clients of FunnyFace Today use handicapped people in their ads. Jane Blum, president of FunnyFace Today, says it is their job to find models who are best suited to fill their clients' requests. For example, if the ad is for a pharmaceutical product, the model should represent a person from the community who has the look of a doctor, patient, nurse, etc., who may use or distribute the product being advertised.

When asked what she looks for in a model, Jane said, "A person with a positive attitude, great vitality, great energy, and professionalism."

Jeffrey Koslow
Models Exchange
2425 Commercial Blvd.
Ft. Lauderdale, FL 33308
305-491-1014
Models Exchange handles many extras for movies and television specials. Commercial print is another strong facet of their business. They are one of southern Florida's oldest nonunion agencies and have provided actors for many films as well as commercials and print. Jeffrey gives the following sound advice for actors:

1. Be available.
2. Be workable (that is, be able to take direction).
3. Use common sense.

Most of Jeffrey's people earn between ten thousand and twenty thousand dollars per year. Some very active people earn more. He suggests that you call his office to set up an appointment or, better still, mail him your headshot.

Debbee May Agency
79 Barrow Street #2A
New York, NY 10014
(212) 633-9821
Debbee May of the Debbee May Agency recommends learning by observing other actors' work. She also feels strongly about developing audition techniques at the audition (other agents recommend being professionally ready before you enter the audition room)

Debbee May runs an active one-woman agency. Her clients use her actors for commercials, print, and films. Casting directors call Debbee for actors to do extra work as well. Like most of the agents I've interviewed, she receives many calls for seniors of all types. Most of her actors are nonunion. Debbee books actors internationally as well.

When asked what she expects in an actor, she said, "It is important for the actor to make a commitment. Go on as many go-sees and auditions as you are called for. That is, spend time doing the work before the actual job." As for training, she feels the most important training is learning by observing. She suggests auditing classes in a drama school (one can audit classes in many schools free of charge). She adds, "You can also learn by going on auditions. No matter how many classes you attend, it may still be difficult to do a cold reading [read in front of people with new material]. The more auditions an actor attends, the more comfortable he or she gets to feel." She finds that "every type really works; it's just a matter of time."

Other advice from Debbee:

1. Show up on time.
2. Be responsible.
3. Look like you're supposed to look on an audition. (Look the part.)
4. Behave like a professional and do the job.

Debbee's commission is 10 percent for extra work (or less, depending on the job); 20 percent for print; 15 to 20 percent for nonunion.

Sherry Lynn
Michele Pommier Models Inc.
1126 Ocean Drive
Miami Beach, FL 33139
(305) 672-9344
Michelle Pommier Models is a "beautiful people" agency. There's one in almost every city.

If you fit the bill, go for it.

This agency is a good one for trim figures and good physiques. (Those workouts may finally pay off.) "Yes, we use some people over sixty," says Sherry Lynn, head of the commercial department. "Actors and models who have what we call the 'mainstream look'—good figures, light hair [gray, blond, or a combination of both]."

The agency has been in business since 1977. Their clients are worldwide and they enjoy a large European market. Models earn about one hundred and fifty dollars per hour (and up). Television commercials are paid union scale (Florida is a right-to-work state).

This agency has several departments (kids, commercial/print, television commercials, and so on). Therefore when you call or send your picture, make sure you direct it to Sherry Lynn.

Here's a word of advice from Sherry: "Never under any circumstances start to do business with any agency who asks for money up front, or an agency registration fee—no way."

David Roos
Gilla Roos Ltd.
16 West 22nd Street
New York, NY 10010
212-727-7820

David Roos of the Gilla Roos agency takes his models under his wing. He has a good eye for salable types and knows how to market them. Among his clients are ad agencies; photographers; graphic designers; and book, catalog, and magazine publishers. He notes, "Clients like to see lots of people. They like to have as many choices as they can because they want to make sure they don't miss anything."

Gilla Roos, David's mother, started this agency in 1974. She had previously been a model and, at age forty-five, went into the agency end of the business. She geared her business toward the mature model.

In 1980, David began working with his mother. He continued the tradition of specializing in working with forty-five-plus models. He notes, "I like working with older people. They have a life experience that shows in their work, and they are generally quite reliable. In the last ten years, the area has grown tremendously." He adds, "There's exciting news happening even now. In addition to trade magazine ads, the pharmaceutical market [which uses many mature people] is heading toward direct consumer advertising. This will provide many more avenues for advertisers to promote their products and additional work for the mature model."

He went on, "We select people who you would believe go to the doctor's office, shop in the supermarket—people who feel comfortable in front of a camera, real people who look good."

In answer to my question about appearance, David said, "A person should be well groomed, carefully made up, and well put together for an interview."

The best way to contact David is to send him your picture. David looks at every photo that comes in. He says, "If you send your picture to five or six agents, and if you are right for the business, someone will discover you."

Here are some final notes from David:

1. Show personality, be outgoing, and be secure.
2. Display some acting ability.
3. Be able to sell yourself.
4. Know how to be camera-ready (makeup, hair, etc.).
5. Be comfortable, look comfortable, and enjoy the shoot.

The William Schill Agency Inc.
250 West 57th Street
New York, NY 10019
(212) 315-5919

After twenty-six years of being a production stage manager, Bill Schill decided to become an agent. Now in *his* second career, Bill heads a very successful agency. He has provided talent for many Broadway, off-Broadway, and regional stages nationwide. Some of his recent film projects include providing people for *What About Bob*, *Jennifer 8*, and *Naked in New York*. On television, Bill has placed actors on many daytime dramas and commercials. He handles more than one hundred actors, and he's always on the lookout for new faces. Bill feels taking classes, contacting casting directors, and networking with people in the business are most important for developing a career.

His office sees people through referrals and is also open to pictures and résumés. Send Bill your headshot. He looks at every photo that comes in.

Casting Offices

Bonita Hofstetter
BHK Arts Consultant Inc.
326 N Street SW
Washington, DC 20024
202-544-0131

Bonita Hofstetter, a casting director, casts for a variety of movies, television programs, and theater. She started casting actors for bit parts and extra work for such acclaimed films as *The Pelican Brief* and *Major League II*.

She loves the work and spends as much time finding the right people for nonspeaking roles as she does for commercials, industrials, television, and theater.

Bonita considers herself a free-lance casting director. After several years of working in Kentucky, Massachusetts, and New York, she was offered a job in Washington, D.C. In 1991 she opened her own office, and to date her credits include *Silent Fall, Jungle Book, Operation Dumbo Drop*, and *The Shadow Conspiracy*.

Bonita finds there is lots of extra work in Washington, D.C. (she covers Baltimore and Richmond as well). There are many medical training films, national educational public service films, and government training films, all of which generally call for mature actors. This is especially true of public service announcements. The types used most often are referred to as "at-home retired" or "casual retired." When Bonita is casting a production, she will advertise in the *Washington Post* in the Friday or Sunday edition.

Wages for extra work vary. Minimum union wage is ninety-four dollars per day. Nonunion workers may earn fifty dollars and up per day.

I asked Bonita what percentage of actors support themselves completely by acting. She replied, "There are about eight hundred and fifty actors here. About three hundred just do acting; the rest generally have some other source of income. A popular fill-in job is doing 'talking books' [books that are recorded for tape]."

Bonita advises actors to mail their headshots and résumés to every casting director, agent, and producer on their list and to attend open auditions. She suggests that you contact her by mail any time you have something to say, such as a résumé update, a new picture, or a change of address, and to keep watching the casting ads in the *Washington Post*.

Sylvia Fay
Sylvia Fay Casting
71 Park Avenue
New York, NY 10016

Sylvia Fay is one of the great ladies of casting. She's been in the business twenty-five years and has cast over one hundred and fifty films. She has cast in Boston and Troy, New York, as well as in New York City.

Her specialties are extras, commercials, and bit parts for feature films. She is a professional, no-nonsense woman and is tops in the business. "I want my people to get the best attention on the set, to have the best places to dress and wait. It's very important to them and to me," she says.

Sylvia finds most of her talent through open calls, which she holds three or four times a year. She sees over fifteen hundred people in a single session. She gives an introductory speech describing the work and what she is looking for, and then she collects the actors' photos and résumés. She also passes out blank cards to the actors so they can provide additional information regarding wardrobe, uniforms, and special abilities.

The biggest difference between principal and extra casting is the quantity of people she has to deal with. She notes, "We do it in bulk. I may need twenty well-dressed people for a party scene or one hundred. I try to get as much realism as possible." Regarding training, she adds, "For extra work, the training needed is to be on the set and learn camera angles."

Mature people are very much part of her casting, and she gets calls for handicapped people, too.

Some of Sylvia's credits include *Law and Order, Reversal of Fortune, Ghost, The Muppets Take Manhattan, Scent of a Woman, A Bronx Tale, Billy Bathgate, Tootsie,* and *Sabrina*. She feels she works with the best staff, including her assistant Fleet Emerson, who has been with her for twenty-four years. Sylvia has seen actors such as Chazz Palminteri and Danny Aiello make the leap from extras and bit parts to feature performers.

Here are some notes from Sylvia:

1. Most important, be on time for a shoot.
2. Be professional; don't be a complainer. Be as pleasant to us as we are to you.
3. Listen to the AD (assistant director), and no one else.
4. Have properly prepared clothes for the scene.
5. Make sure your résumé includes volunteer work, interests, and hobbies.

Her final tip: "Get out there and do it."

Grant Wilfley
Wilfley/Todd Casting
60 Madison Avenue
New York, NY 10010
212-685-3537
This casting office is one of the few that cast the entire package, that is, extras to principals. As with most casting directors, they welcome newcomers and *absolutely* use mature people.

Grant Wilfley likes to be contacted by mail versus phone calls. Send him your headshot and résumé for the initial contact. Then follow up with picture postcards on a regular basis.

For extra work, Grant suggests that you send a note along with your picture and résumé to the effect of, "I'm available for extra work." He explains, "Your picture may come in just when we need your type."

The agency also keeps "special" files. Grant says, "Make sure you list any special wardrobe [gowns, tuxedos, furs, etc.], uniforms, or anything new that may be of interest. The more files you're in, the better." (You may send duplicate photos, with a note attached, after you have made your initial contact.)

Grant recommends that you always include your résumé with duplicate photos. "Sometimes we want an extra whom we will be able to upgrade," he says. The résumés help him match appropriate actors with each part.

Here are some additional notes from Grant:

1. Be aware of what's going on.
2. Don't get in the way.
3. Stay where you are assigned.
4. Be professional.
5. Don't ask too many questions, and don't chat with people who are working.

Additional Information Pertinent to Your Local Market

Atlanta, GA
Agents' offices generally house information (flyers, brochures, etc.) on production, workshops, and seminars. Georgia is a right-to-work state; the pay is generally the same for union as it is for nonunion.

Boston, MA
It is possible to work in Boston without being listed with an agency, though agents here may provide access to print work and film (nonunion as well as union). Actors should send pictures and résumés to several franchised or legitimate nonfranchised

agencies. There are a number of Boston agents and casting directors listed in Appendix B, and AFTRA and SAG offices maintain lists as well.

It is also a good idea to contact corporate and production houses who do their own casting (check the trade papers and telephone directory for names). Send pictures and résumés to these firms, and follow up with a phone call requesting an appointment.

Chicago, IL

Chicago has a more than respectable corporate market. Most of the union work is AFTRA, and there's also quite a bit of nonunion production. Actors can list with several agents.

Dallas, TX

Dallas gets a good portion of film and television production, but the work is sporadic. Most films that may be set in other southern states are actually filmed in and around Dallas. When films do come to town, locals get a lot of work. Check often with SAG and AFTRA, and watch for announcements in the *Dallas Observer*.

The commercial market is quite big. Many advertising agencies are headquartered here or have branch offices that create original productions. Check *Dallas Actors' Handbook* to find out which production companies and corporations keep in-house casting files. Some casting directors have general auditions or interviews, which would be announced in the trade publications.

Texas is a right-to-work state, which means that nonunion actors have much opportunity to work there. You absolutely need an agent (even nonunion actors are better off with agents).

Los Angeles, CA

Los Angeles is the world capital of moviemaking and television production. The business here is especially hard on women and older people. However, they are always looking for new faces. There are commercials and print being shot here. Contact casting directors and agents. The vast majority of commercials are cast through agents. For current updates, *The Agencies*, available at bookshops, updates its lists monthly.

Miami and Fort Lauderdale, FL

Southern Florida is seeing continuous growth. Many European production companies shoot in South Florida, and quite a few network television shows pass through for an episode or two and sometimes more. With so much film production in the area, there's always extra work, most of which is non-SAG. Additionally, there's enough on-camera and print work to make a very strong market. When it gets cold up North, things get busy down South. Interested actors should send pictures and résumés to casting directors and agents, along with a note expressing their availability for work.

Minneapolis and St. Paul, MN

When films come to town, extra and day-player roles get cast; sometimes, actors have a chance to audition for supporting roles as well. Extra calls are announced in the newspaper. You can also let casting directors know you're available. Send pictures and résumés to them, or, better yet, drop by in person and introduce yourself. Nonunion actors are usually called directly by casting directors, so it's especially important that you make yourself known.

New York, NY

There are well over a hundred talent agencies (and more than half as many casting companies) in the New York area. Finding representation often requires staying in touch with the agents who express interest in you. Appendix B lists many of them. However, for current updates, check *Ross Reports Television*, a monthly publication that lists agents and casting directors.

Philadelphia, PA

In this town, it's to your advantage to contact both casting directors and agents. Agents get some work casting directors don't, and casting directors get some work agents don't.

Phoenix, AZ

Phoenix is growing in commercial television and print work.

Contact the agents and casting directors, and keep in touch with them. The SAG office has lists of agents and casting directors. These are updated monthly.

San Francisco, CA
It is very necessary to have an agent here. Most casting directors are too busy to call actors directly. However, actors should still send pictures and résumés to casting directors for their files. It may not do much good, but it can't hurt.

Seattle, WA
Seattle's corporate and commercial markets are pretty evenly split between union (primarily AFTRA) and nonunion production. Actors can market themselves directly to casting directors.

Washington, DC (Maryland, Virginia)
There's little distinction between casting directors and talent agents here, and the terms "casting company" and "casting agency" are used interchangeably. There are additional companies that work primarily with models. The market is quite strong for older models.

7

Publications and Organizations
Staying Hands-On

Subscribing to a weekly or monthly publication provides current and valuable information for the actor. Many publications supply updated listings of local agents and casting directors, casting notices, and announcements of seminars and other pertinent events. Some have interviews or bits of information about ad agencies, agents, and casting directors. In any event, reading one regularly will help make you a well-informed actor.

Since it would take an entire book to list every publication pertaining to show business, I have chosen a few as representative. Also included are examples of hot lines and professional organizations. To help you make a selection, a brief description is included with each listing. A few are national, many are regional.

National

The Hollywood Reporter is published in Los Angeles and read by those who want to keep up with who's who in the industry and stay well informed about current and upcoming productions.

Backstage, published in New York, has good coverage of current information concerning commercial productions in many areas of the country (the sections are divided geographically).

Madison Avenue Handbook is a resource guide for models. It features names, addresses, and phone numbers of agents and casting directors in most cities in the United States. There are also listings of Canadian agencies and much more.

Model News and *Show Business News* are both monthly publications. They cover news of the industry nationally. Both are published by John King Productions, New York.

Henderson Enterprises, a publisher in New York, provides up-to-date mailing labels for agents and casting directors in Los Angeles, Florida, Atlanta, Boston, Chicago, and New York. These labels help to make mailings a snap and might even offer additional names for *your* mailing lists.

For further details relative to the above, see the following listings under New York and Los Angeles.

Boston, MA

Publications

The Boston Phoenix. Available at some newsstands in the Boston area. A weekly newspaper that includes audition notices. Published on Fridays.

Casting News, P. O. Box 201, Boston, MA 02134, (617) 787-2991. Available by subscription or at a number of newsstands in Boston and Cambridge and at some suburban outlets. Published twice a month. Includes resources, articles, actor and musician auditions, and more.

Organizations

StageSource, One Boylston Place, Boston, MA 02116, (617) 423-2475. A resource and service organization for actors and other theater professionals. Services include a casting hot line, picture and résumé file, a nontraditional casting file, and workshops. StageSource publishes *The Source*.

International Television Association (ITVA), 26 Constitution Drive, Southborough, MA 01772, (508)890-4882. Committed to the needs of the professional video communicator. Actors find the workshops and meetings offer good networking opportunities.

New England Producers Association, 1380 Soldiers Field Road, Boston, MA, 02135, (617) 698-6372. Publishes a newsletter called *The Slate*, which includes a column called

"The Actor's Corner." They keep members up-to-date. Their actor/director workshops are open to NEPA members and nonmembers and are announced on AFTRA/SAG and StageSource hot lines.

Chicago

Publications

Act One Reports, 2632 North Lincoln Avenue, Chicago, IL 60614, (312) 348-4658. A booklet that can be purchased at bookstores. Updated approximately three times a year. Provides contact information for Chicago-area agents, casting directors, union officials, production companies, ad agencies, and Chicago and Midwest theaters. A must for newcomers.
Acting and Modeling Resource Guide to Chicago, by Don Kaufman (Chicago: self-published). Available at bookstores. Updated yearly. Contains lists of instructors, agents, casting directors, employment agencies, and more.
Audition News, Chicago Entertainment Co., 6272 West North Avenue, Chicago, IL 60639, (312) 637-4695. Available by subscription or at retail outlets. Published monthly. This trade magazine contains lists of agents and casting directors, ads for photographers and classes, etc.
Chicago Reader, 11 East Illinois, Chicago, IL 60611, (312) 828-0350. Available at retail outlets, street-corner boxes, and this address. This free weekly general-interest newspaper is also a source of audition information. Published on Thursdays; check the "wanted" section of the classifieds.
Performink, 2632 North Lincoln Avenue, Chicago, IL 60614, (312) 348-4658. Available by subscription or can be picked up free of charge at agents' offices, theater lobbies, and the Act 1 bookstore. It provides casting notices and news of the industry. Published biweekly.

Organizations

Illinois Film Office, (312) 427-3456. The IFO primarily announces calls for extras and stand-ins.

Columbia College Department of Film and Video, 600 South Michigan Avenue, Chicago, IL 60605, (312) 663-1600. Actors interested in participating in student projects can post their names and phone numbers on the eighth-floor bulletin board.

Dallas

Dallas Actors' Handbook. Available at bookstores like B. Dalton and Taylors and at the Dallas Public Library. Updated every year or so. Lists agents, casting directors, theaters, photographers, teachers, and so forth. Tells which corporate producers, production houses, and ad agencies accept pictures and résumés. Includes a glossary of stage and screen terms.

Dallas Observer. Available at supermarkets, street-corner boxes, etc. Free weekly paper. Includes audition notices (nonunion).

Los Angeles

On Production and Post Production, 17337 Ventura Blvd., Encino, CA 91316, (818) 907-6682. Available by subscription. Covers information about feature films and television commercials.

The Agencies, P. O. Box 44, Hollywood, CA 90078. Available by subscription or at Samuel French and at Larry Edmunds Bookshops. Updated monthly. Lists information about every agency, including the names of agents and subagents, with a line or two of useful commentary per entry.

Drama-logue, P. O. Box 38771, Los Angeles, CA 90038, (213) 464-5079. Available by subscription and at newsstands all over town. Published weekly. Contains reviews, articles, ads, and casting notices, including nonunion commercial calls.

Hollywood Reporter, P. O. Box 38771, Los Angeles, CA 90078. Good industry news. Published daily. At newsstands and by subscription.

Minneapolis and St. Paul

Publications

Spotlight, 3120 Hennepin Avenue, South Suite 404, Minneapolis MN 55408, (612) 823-3719. Distributed free at theaters and other Twin Cities locations. Monthly publication that carries film industry news as well as theater and music news. Features articles, interviews, and a few casting notices.
Star Tribune. The Sunday edition's classified section includes casting notices and is a primary source of casting information. Can be bought on newsstands.

Organizations

Film Board Production hot line, (612) 333-0436.
Announces who's casting films shooting in the area.

Miami, FL (Southern and Central)

Publications

In the absence of local trade papers, the following are good sources for casting notices:

The Miami Herald, Friday "weekend" section.
Sun Sentinal, Showtime section.
New Times. Published on Wednesdays.

Organizations

Professional Actors Association of Florida (PAAF), P. O. Box 610366, Miami Beach, FL 33161-0366, (305) 932-1427. PAAF is a nonprofit organization for Florida-based actors. Activities include workshops, a member talent directory, and a car-pool hot line. Membership requirements include a two-year union membership, Florida residency (six months to one year), and three speaking parts under union contract. Nonmembers may participate in workshops and auditions.

Unions

> Screen Actors Guild (SAG), 7300 North Kendall Drive, Suite 620, Miami, FL 33156, (305) 670-7677.
>
> American Federation of Television and Radio Artists (AFTRA), 20401 NW 2nd Avenue, Suite 102, Miami, FL 33169, (305) 652-4842.

Both unions maintain a current listing of agents and casting directors. These lists are also available to nonunion people. Local telephone directories list talent agents and model agents as well.

New York City

Back Stage, 1515 Broadway, New York, NY 10036, (212) 764-7300. Available at newsstands and by mail subscription at this address. Published each Thursday. The oldest and best established of the trade papers. Probably the primary source of audition information and casting notices for most actors.

New York Casting, 135 East 65th Street, New York, NY 10021, (212) 472-6585. Available at newsstands or by mail subscription and is also distributed free to several performers' organizations. Published biweekly. Includes, in addition to casting notices, lists of agents, casting directors, and production houses. Geared primarily toward people in transition into the professional performing arts.

Ross Reports Television, Television Index Inc., 40-29 27th Street, Long Island City, NY 11101, (718) 937-3900. Available at bookstores, magazine shops, drama shops, etc. Updated monthly. This booklet provides casting information for New York and Los Angeles television shows and New York commercial producers, talent agents, and casting directors.

Show Business News, John King Productions, 244 Madison Avenue, New York, NY 10016. Available at newsstands and by subscription at this address. Published monthly. Covers the news of the industry. Lists agents, casting directors, producers, photographers, etc., nationally.

Model News, John King Productions, 244 Madison Avenue, New York, NY 10016. Available at newsstands and by subscription at this address. Published monthly. Nationally covers agents, producers, photographers, news of the model industry, and much more.

Henderson's Mailing Labels, Henderson Enterprises, 360 East 65th Street, 15E, New York, NY 10021, (212) 472-2292. Provides preaddressed labels for agents and casting directors. Most sets are priced at five to eight dollars (up to twenty dollars), depending on size.

Seattle

There is no local trade paper. The following newspapers are worth checking, although none are complete sources of audition information:

Seattle Post-Intelligencer. See Friday's "Auditions" column.
Seattle Weekly. See the "Call-Board" column.
Seattle Times. See the Thursday classifieds.

Washington, DC

Publications

The *Washington Post.* Audition notices run in the Friday edition's Weekend section, and sometimes in the Sunday papers.
The City Paper. Available at food stores, drugstores, street-corner boxes, all over town. A free weekly (Thursdays). Includes audition listings, reviews, and a want-ad column in the back.

Organizations

Actors Center, P. O. Box 50180, Washington, DC 20091, (206) 638-3777. This service organization provides members with an audition hot line and newsletter. Attending their workshops held every Saturday morning is a good way to meet people and network. Members can call Monday afternoons from 2:00–6:00 and Wednesdays and Fridays from 10:00–2:00. Highly recommended, especially for newcomers.

Backstage Books, 2101 P Street, NW, Washington, DC 20037, (206) 775-1488. One wall of the shop area posts the *Washington Post* audition notices; another wall lists student films, showcase auditions, and more. A third wall displays business-card and advertising services (photography, instructions, etc.)

Also see Appendix B for listings of SAG/AFTRA offices and Appendix C for names and addresses of agents and casting directors.

Keeping in touch gives you an edge. Most probably, it will increase your opportunity for work and heighten your professionalism.

8

Schools and
Training Programs
Pros and Cons

There are modeling and acting schools across the country that cover every aspect of the profession. Since the immediate goals are print modeling, extra work, and commercials, I will discuss types of schools available, provide guidelines for locating and selecting one, and suggest a program that would serve your best interests.

I personally feel that a good class can be valuable, especially in the beginning. Besides perfecting camera techniques, etc., it is another means of meeting people in the business. The teachers may have contacts with local businesses, casting directors, and agents to whom they can recommend you send your picture and résumé.

Most major cities and quite a few smaller ones have professional schools that provide classes, programs, and seminars in commercial acting. While some are taught through universities and colleges, many are private and conducted by actor-teachers who know their craft and are aware of the pitfalls.

Most schools advertise in the trade papers (see Chapter 7). The telephone directory yellow pages also lists schools. Appropriate headings include "Acting," "Modeling," "Television and Film," "Commercial Acting," etc.

Rather than recommend specific schools in each part of the country, I'll list some guidelines for finding the best classes available.

Should you decide to take a course, make sure it's a legitimate school that is primarily interested in you rather than just your money. You may want to check them out with the Better Business Bureau or your local chamber of commerce. Try to check with former mature students and see what their impressions are. The following guidelines should help you to choose a reputable school.

1. Look for a school that doesn't make wild promises of success.
2. Shun an ad agency that guarantees you'll make big money in six months. No one has any idea of how much money you'll make or when.
3. Take heed of ads that read "We can get you into commercials" or promise that you will become a model. They *can't* promise; it doesn't work that way.
4. Beware of a school that says you'll receive a letter of recommendation. No casting director will consider you for work just because you have a letter of recommendation.

Call the schools that say they are trained to teach you about the industry and to develop your craft. When you call, find out what the class covers, how much on-camera training you get, when the class meets, how much it costs, and the number of students in each class (the smaller the better). Check to see if guest speakers in the business are invited to lecture. Then choose several classes and ask if and when you may audit them.

It is important to choose a program that will serve your best interests. While most schools will agree that it is less important for a mature model to attend modeling school, there are always some benefits to be derived from attending one. These include learning modeling techniques and learning the basis of good grooming. You may find that these are qualities you already possess. But for many, these characteristics must be acquired or perhaps improved upon.

Before you enroll, ask yourself exactly what you expect to gain by doing so. If you enter knowing your goal, a good modeling school can be a first step in the right direction. It may also provide a few contacts and an objective personal evaluation. In this case, a modeling school might be a good way to start your career.

For example, Scott Powers Productions, in New York, recently developed a course geared specifically toward commercial print modeling. Scott comes highly recommended by working models such as Joan Lowry, Bill Bowdren, Bea DeLizio, and Larry O'Brien. They all agree that this course provided them with additional tools for success. It might help you, too.

If, on the other hand, you want to zero in on commercials, it is advisable to seek out a class that specializes in the field—one that would provide information about the business, teach you on-camera techniques, and give you an opportunity to practice in front of the camera.

Viola Harris, an actress who resumed her career at age sixty, has this to say: "It is most important to take an acting course of any kind so that you don't enter an audition cold. Taking a course helps you as a performer and gives you confidence. If you have that, you are well on your way."

9

Unions

To Join or Not to Join

SAG and AFTRA

Two primary unions are involved in commercials and film: Screen Actors Guild (SAG) and American Federation of Television and Radio Artists (AFTRA). They are both part of the Associated Actors and Artists of America (Four A's), which also include Actors' Equity Association (AEA), the American Guild of Musical Artists (AGMA), and the American Guild of Variety Artists (AGVA). SAG is also a member of the International Federation of Actors (IFA), a global organization of performers' unions.

SAG has jurisdiction over work that is filmed (television commercials, motion pictures, industrial and educational films) and AFTRA covers work on audio- and videotape (television and radio commercials, television and radio programs, slide films, industrial films recorded on videotape, and phonograph recordings). Since most commercials are shot on film, SAG is of much greater concern to the commercial actor than AFTRA.

History of the Union

Prior to unions, actors were lucky to be paid fifteen dollars for a long day's work or sixty-six dollars for a six-day week. The unregulated hours and working conditions were even worse than the pay. There was no concern for safety and environmental conditions, and no time for meals. To make matters worse, producers declared a 50 percent pay cut for all actors under studio contract. With no organization or collective bargaining power, the actors had no choice but to take the cut.

Shortly thereafter, a small group of actors met to consider creating a union for actors. They filed the necessary legal papers, and after a four-year struggle the union finally received recognition. On May 9, 1937, SAG had its first contract with producers.

What Can the Unions Do for Me?

Unions provide actors with the following benefits.

1. They see that you are paid properly and promptly.
2. In addition to basic pay, the Guild contract provides payments for overtime, holidays, travel time, fittings, and wardrobe.
3. SAG requires the producers to supply meals, meal breaks, and overall good working conditions.
4. SAG provides an attractive pension and health plan. Performers who earn a minimum SAG income of $5,000 per year are automatically enrolled for twelve months in the health plan, which also covers your spouse and dependent children. Dental benefits and life insurance are also included. If you earn more than $2,000 a year in SAG employment for at least ten years, you will qualify for a Guild pension upon retirement.

These valuable benefits are paid for entirely by the employer. SAG members do not contribute to the pension and health plan.

The Right Time to Join

The union may play a significant part in the professional actor's life. However, there are actors (especially those who do their major work in print) who enjoy an active and rewarding career while remaining nonunion. According to several nonunion actors I've spoken with, the consensus seems that they are quite satisfied with the way their careers are going. Patricia Veliotes, a nonunion actress in Washington, D.C., says, "I never find a lack of work." Bill Bowdren, an actor/model you met in Chapter 1, states, "I get more work being nonunion." The mature actor who is new to the business should note that union talent cannot work a nonunion project without all sorts of special dispensations. And that is why Patricia and Bill aren't union. However, others I've talked with are looking forward to becoming union members or have already done so. Malcolm Beers, a New York actor, says, "I'd love to get into SAG and make money while I'm in the shower." Stephen Lewis, a Washington, D.C., actor, plans on joining as soon as possible.

How Do I Become a Member?

It is much easier to join AFTRA than SAG. You may join AFTRA by filling out a membership application and paying your initial fee, which at this writing is $842.50, plus dues, which are $42.50 semiannually. That's all it takes, and you are a member of a professional acting union.

SAG is a little more complicated. In order to protect its members, the union has made the requirements more difficult.

You may join SAG if you have been a member of AFTRA (or any affiliated union) for one year and have worked at least once as a principal performer in that union's jurisdiction (a principal performer in a commercial is anyone who is on-camera and is identified with the product, demonstrates the product, or reacts to the message; you don't necessarily have to speak lines). You may also join if you have worked three days as an extra under SAG jurisdiction or have performed in a principal role in a SAG film or commercial. If you meet these requirements, paying the initial fee of $1,008 and the semiannual basic dues of $42.50 makes you a member in good standing.

If you are a paid-up member of an affiliated performers' union such as AFTRA, SAG will lower the semiannual dues to 37.50. For more details about the unions, contact their offices. See

Appendix C for SAG and AFTRA branch offices throughout the country.

Remember, you don't need to make any decision immediately. Nonunion as well as union commercials and commercial extra work are produced in most parts of the country, including major cities. You may not need to join a union. My suggestion: wait and see.

10

Talking with the Pros

There's nothing like getting the lowdown straight from the horse's mouth. For this very reason, I've chosen several actors whose special tips, although unique, have been repeated by many. In general, most actors operate their business in a similar manner. However, they all have their favorite ingredient for a "running start."

Those interviewed come from a variety of backgrounds, cover a broad range of types, and are quite committed to their work. The following are representative of the men and women I've talked with. A few facts before we begin:

1. All are working model/actors.
2. Most are quite satisfied with the direction of their career.
3. Some work more often than others, due to opportunity or choice.
4. Their individual yearly incomes range from $5000 to $70,000.
5. Their ages range from fifty to seventy.
6. Most have some additional income to augment the inconsistency of work.
7. All were very willing to share the special tips that they find make the difference.

Rejection: An Attitude
Bea Delizio
Long Island, New York
Age 65
Bea stresses the necessity of being able to handle rejection. Unfortunately, rejection is very much a part of the business. If it's not put in its place, it can color your attitude and undermine

your confidence. Bea advises, "Realize it's nothing personal. There are many reasons why you're not chosen. Something as simple as your hair color or your facial features might have reminded the client of his ex-wife, or you were just not the type they decided on this time."

Bea doesn't consider herself a performer. However, after she started working in the field, she was not only hooked, but knew for sure this is what she wanted to do. She says, "This business changed my life. It made me more assertive. I found I had more in me than I knew. I meet people like myself. I've made lovely friends. I get a thrill out of other people getting a kick out of seeing me."

Bea is not completely financially dependent on her career. She does have some great months, but there are some lean ones too. However, she finds it gets better each year. She concludes, "I have my golf, my country club. I bowl, and I work as much as I can. What you do is what you get."

Getting Down to Brass Tacks

Larry O'Brien
New York
Age 62

Larry, a former horse trainer, calls attention to the fact that "show business is called a business, because that's what it is." He explains, "Models and the people who work in commercials are self-employed. You do not find regular employment with one boss, earning a weekly or monthly salary. You dispatch mailings, audition, go on go-sees, to land as many jobs as possible. You are constantly looking for work." Most important, says Larry, is to be aware that this is a business—treat it as such; be professional.

Larry also feels quite strongly about taking classes. He notes, "Every time you get in front of a camera in class helps you to maintain an edge when you audition."

His one complaint is the cold New York weather. "Cold weather is painful; hot is just uncomfortable." But there's no stopping Larry. He's planning on moving to Dallas soon and continuing his career there, where it's warm.

You've Got to Be There, Get There, and You're On

Stephen Lewis

Stephen Lewis
Washington, D.C.
Age range 55–60
Stephen recommends making availability your number one priority, especially in the early stages of your career. When the agents and casting directors find they can depend on you to get to the auditions and go-sees, then you might become *their* number one priority.

Stephen recommends including the words "I'm available" when you send out your regular mailings. However, when you are away or unavailable, it would be most wise to advise everyone of this. In this case, he suggests that you send a picture postcard to your mailing list with a message stating, "I'm out of town and will be available for work again on [a specific date]." Stephen's last bit of advice: "Keep making contacts. You can't sit around waiting for the phone to ring."

There's No Gain Without Pain

Bill Bowdren
Ridgefield, Connecticut
Age 59
Bill, a former marketing executive, calls attention to the fact

Bill
Bowdren

that modeling and acting in commercials is a lifetime activity. You can enter the field at seventeen or seventy.

Bill markets himself as a proactive adult who takes reasonably good care of himself. He does a lot of health care ads, and when he is called by an agent for a pharmaceutical, he not only will question the agent about the product, but he also will go to his local pharmacy, look for the medication (or a similar one), and check with the pharmacist to understand fully what the product does. For example, when his agent called him about a medication for high blood pressure, Bill's research revealed that the medication reduces pressure and reduces incident of stroke. Bill explains how this additional knowledge helps him: "In my mind I have high blood pressure. I take it . . . it's good stuff. It makes me feel good. I get these facts in my head, then I can approach the job with an added edge." Bill goes that extra mile—and it works.

Energy Is Where It's At

Patricia Veliotes
Washington, D.C.
Age 63

Patricia advises, "Be up, but not on, not forced or phony. They can always ask you to tone down your reading, but they won't ask you to inject a little life into it. They'll merely assume you have no vitality or are too nervous to show it."

For go-sees and auditions, Patricia works on getting her adrenaline going. She gets lots of energy into her expressions (not *too* much) as well as her voice. She notes, "Take your cue from the director, listen carefully, do what he says, then go all the way."

At this writing, Patricia considers herself a part-time actress (her husband's business takes them out of the country several months a year). When he retires in two years, Patricia plans to go full speed ahead. When she makes the switch from a part-time to a full-time actress, Patricia plans to "make rounds regularly, call the hot line more often [Actors Center in Washington, D.C.], keep in constant touch with central casting in Washington, D.C., and Baltimore. This job is what you make of it."

Luck and a Bit of Know-How Certainly Help

Patti Karr
New York
Age range 55–60
Patti hails from Texas. She danced her way to New York and Broadway. Patti isn't our typical "second career" actress, but her work in commercials started only a few years ago.

Before she became a member of SAG, she landed her first commercial. She says, "I was lucky; it turned out to be a big one. It was a national and a series of five different ones for the same product." Since then, commercials have been a major part of Patti's career. She explains, "I recently did several back-to-back. I was really on a roll . . . and then nothing . . . that's the business." Patti's special tip is to be "prepared." Keep a good variety of clothing in your closet. When you go on an audition, always carry a bag containing accessories (glasses, scarf, cap, extra top, and so on). There have been times when having glasses or a colored scarf made the difference.

Making Rounds, It's Part of the Game

Nella Griffin
Queens, New York
Age range 50–60
Nella finds rounds to be a most essential ingredient for her career. "There's nothing like personal contact," she says. "Why, a few times I even struck it lucky. I landed the jobs because the casting director whom I visited happened to be looking for just my type."

Nella Griffin

Of course, more often than not, the person you want to see may be unavailable. In that case, Nella suggests you leave your headshot and résumé (or picture postcard) with a note to the effect of, "Sorry I missed you. I will call in a few days to set up an appointment."

Another valuable tip from Nella is, always learn the name of the receptionist. Saying "Hello, Susan" may get your phone call through more readily. She also advocates quite strongly that you be polite and friendly, since today's receptionist may be tomorrow's casting director. You never know.

These special tips on rejection, business, availability, going that extra mile, showing vitality, taking accessories in your bag, and making the rounds are the added pointers that have made a difference in many careers. They may also make a difference in yours.

11

Brave New Worlds
Industrials, Voice-Overs,
and Cable Television

The parameters of the world of show business have been expanding both quantitatively and qualitatively, creating opportunities that never would have been anticipated a decade ago. This development has been spurred on by changes in technology, corporate persona, and marketing practices, and by opportunities for career expansion. Joan Greenspan, Screen Actors Guild's national director of industrial/educational contracts, says, "The field is in its very early stages; it is too early to tell where the market is headed. To date, however, there is a multiplicity of platforms with many stairs. It is evident that the technological expansion is creating a broader area of opportunity for the performer."

Opportunities for performers in this burgeoning field include not only speaking parts for on-camera, voice-over, and narration, but extra work and jobs for people with specific looks and special skills. For example, one useful skill is being proficient in a technical field or vocabulary, especially in computers, medicine, or the pharmaceutical industry. Furthermore, if you understand technical terminology or medical terms, you could be an excellent candidate for above-scale income. Fluency in a foreign language may prove valuable as well. The demand for people with this ability is continually growing, especially for multilingual educational training films, tapes, and point-of-purchase material. Spanish is the most wanted tongue, followed by other Romance and Asian languages.

Industrials

The timing is excellent for pursuing industrials. With the increase in new technology, industrials have become more popular marketing strategies and therefore provide broader outlets for the performer. Corporations and educational and religious organizations use industrials to demonstrate, inform, and teach, utilizing the latest in communications technology.

Today, industrials include corporate image pieces shown to a broad general public; traditional films; and motivational, sales, and informational material—all produced by corporations large and small. There are point-of-purchase videos, which are prerecorded informational videos designed primarily to sell or promote specific products or services. In a department store, the point-of-purchase video is shown at the counter or spot where the merchandise is being sold. Additionally, there are interactive videos; tape cut-ins for live teleconferences (sometimes global via satellite uplink); and laser disc, CDI (Compact Disc Interactive), and CD-ROM recordings. In short, industrials include anything and everything that can go on tape, film, or disc but isn't made for commercials, theater, or television.

CD-ROM and CDI are sprouting technologies with huge potential for the performer. These are computer-compatible compact discs (including laser discs) that can deliver both audio and video. CDIs are used in consumer products such as games, which can include live actors. CD-ROM software is capable of reproducing full-motion pictures.

Where Are the Jobs for Industrials?

Finding the jobs in nonbroadcast venues varies a bit by region. New York City is said to have the busiest corporate market encompassing live, film, and video industrials. The union jobs are pretty evenly split between AFTRA and SAG. There is also a lively nonunion market.

Industrials are often cast through agents, although casting notices appear in the trades as well. Most times it's best to work with agents who specialize in this market. Actors can also market themselves directly. Lists of industrial production houses and corporations with in-house facilities are found in *Ross Reports Television* and in the trades.

Chicago has a more-than-respectable corporate market. Most union work is AFTRA, and there's also quite a bit of nonunion production. Generally, one agent covers all fields. However, the nonbroadcast arena is so big that some agencies have a separate nonbroadcast department. Some corporations and production companies have staff members who handle casting in-house. These are listed in *Act One Reports*.

Dallas is a popular relocation area. Many corporations have opened headquarters there, which has resulted in increased corporate film and video production opportunities.

The nonbroadcast field is not limited to these major production centers. San Francisco, Seattle, Los Angeles, Denver, Detroit, Minneapolis, Atlanta, Miami, Washington, D.C., Boston, Nashville, and many points between have multiple producers working in nonbroadcast.

Nonunion markets dominate in many parts of the country. For union and nonunion work in nonbroadcast venues, list with commercial agents and market yourself directly. A number of production companies accept pictures and résumés. Check the trade papers and publications, and watch the ads in your local paper.

Preparing for the Shoot

If you are hired for a speaking part in an industrial, prepare your script as you would for a commercial. A particular aspect of nonbroadcast productions is that more often than not, speaking roles will deal with more complex copy (technical, medical, mechanical, etc.). Therefore, special attention must be paid to the terminology and pronunciation.

When the job is yours, I would suggest that as soon as you get the copy (which should be a few days before the shoot), you examine the script to see if it contains any specialized vocabulary or high-tech language. Refer to a good dictionary. You will want to find a good bookstore or library that has access to technical dictionaries (medical, computer, etc.) You will find them very handy.

Learn the terminology and pronunciation. Practice the words till they roll off your tongue like a part of your everyday language. Then proceed to practice reading the copy until you are able to deliver the lines smoothly, believably, and with interest (see Chapter 5).

Tools for Industrials

The TelePrompTer Because the copy for industrials can sometimes be complex, most industrial shoots employ the use of a TelePrompTer. This most welcomed aid eliminates the need to memorize the script. The TelePrompTers are set up in the studio and placed so the actor can view them easily. The copy is televised onto the screens and scrolled along by the TelePrompTer operator. Then the actor reads the lines as they appear on the screen. There's generally a fair amount of copy, so you should have a good understanding of the copy and be very familiar with it. Using the TelePrompTer provides the actor with an additional tool for a smooth presentation in front of the camera.

The Earprompter The earprompter, another valuable aid, is a relatively new system. Like the TelePrompTer, it eliminates the need to memorize. Also, last-minute changes are easy to make. On the other hand, earprompters aren't easy to use. In fact, according to Bob Spiro, associate executive director of New York AFTRA, "Some people use them very well and some people can't use them at all."

A professional earprompter consists of a small tape recorder, a wireless neck loop (worn under your clothes), an earpiece with a volume control, and sometimes a hand-held button. Here's how it works. First, you record your lines on a tape recorder. Then, when it's time to perform, you play the lines back through a hidden earphone, reciting the words as you hear them.

Because the earpiece is custom-made to fit entirely within your particular ear, it is considered personal equipment and is owned by the actor. Check the yellow pages and/or ask other actors for the name of a hearing-aid specialist who can fit one for you.

However, before you spend your money, test it first to see if it will work for you. Practice with a makeshift arrangement. Record a few minutes of copy on a cassette tape recorder, play it back using earphones, and recite the words as you hear them. Practice the same piece several times until you get comfortable. This takes lots of practice, so don't get discouraged.

As you improve, walk and gesture as you speak. In the beginning, you probably will sound a bit mechanical. Work for spontaneity. Eventually, you should be able to deliver the lines more naturally.

Several actors I've spoken with find it to be a superb piece of equipment. Others in the field have suggested that the earprompter is instrumental in getting work. However, when I asked Bob Spiro if he found that producers were influenced by an actor's having a earprompter, he replied, "No, not really. The actor is chosen for his talent, looks, etc. If he can handle the earprompter well and it helps to better his performance, then using one would be to his advantage. [But] he's not going to lose the job because he doesn't have one."

AFTRA's and SAG's regional offices offer periodic training seminars in using earprompters. Private training through commercial acting classes may also be available.

The Shoot

The call might be for one to three days of work. Generally, the shoot starts at 9:00 A.M. and is scheduled to last until 5:00 P.M. You may be a spokesperson or you may have a scene or an extra job in a training film. In most cases, your own clothes will be called for. If there are any specific uniforms or special outfits needed, they will be taken care of by wardrobe. The shoot may be on location or in a studio, and the former might call for odd hours. (In retail stores, shoots will almost always be before or after business hours; in hospitals, the shoot generally takes place off-hours in an inactive area.) In a nurses' training film I shot, we worked from 9:00 P.M. until 5:00 A.M. in the laboratory testing section. We finished the shoot just before the area started bustling with hospital activity.

The Money

The union scale for on-camera work (tape or film) in general industrials is a one-day minimum of $380. Point-of-purchase film or tape is $472. Weekly rates are $1,333 and $1,651, respectively. A half-day rate (four hours or less) is 65 percent of the day rate. Under both unions, the on-camera scale for interactive media agreements is $504 for a day player, $1,276 for three days, and $1,752 for a week. As with other AFTRA and SAG contracts, pension and health plan payments and the agent's percentage are added to the minimums.

According to Back Stage, at least 50 percent of nonbroadcast work is nonunion. Reputable producers will pay at or near union scale, though without union benefits. With most corporations the reason behind their using nonunion talent isn't the money. They are either antiunion or don't want to be bothered.

Voice-Overs

The search is on for new voice-over talent. Clients want to hear new voices, the advertising agencies are more open to hiring women performers, and new technology is creating additional opportunities. However, the voice-over market is still highly competitive.

Why Choose Voice-Overs?

Many people pursue the voice-over market for the following reasons.

Money Voice-overs are most lucrative. According to Charles Cowing of the J. Michael Bloom Agency, "In three hours, people can do six to eight spots and make thousands of dollars." Deborah Gear, a voice-over actress, knows people in the business who live extremely well. She adds, "There are guys out there living in beautiful homes in the suburbs working three days a week who make $400,000 a year." Deborah Gear is relatively new in the business and is building her voice-over career. She gets anywhere from $275 to $1,000 a session.

Anonymity Some people love to perform but hesitate to face a camera. As a voice-over performer, you can hide behind your anonymity and just be a voice. Ellene Faison, a voice-over performer, actress, and teacher, makes the following comment: "No one sees you, your physical appearance is not important. . . . It's your voice that sells the product." Deborah Gear, whose first career was modeling, finds voice-over work to be a dream come true. She explains, "The first time I went into a soundproof booth I felt like Miss America on "Twenty Questions." It was heaven because nobody could see me. The only thing they concerned themselves with was my voice." Before she was in a business where she was always picked apart (her hair, eyes, weight, etc.), but now she can focus her attention completely on the words of the copy and how it will sound. Tom Perkins, a recording engineer, adds, "When you hear someone and then you see what they look like, you say, I never expected that kind of voice from that little guy. The only thing that matters is your voice."

Talent Many people come into the business because they've been told they have interesting voices or their voices sound different. They may have unusual accents, rhythm, or pitch.

Arnold Stang built a career by developing a character with a funny high voice. (He was best known for his Chunky Chocolates ads.) Anne Meara and Jerry Stiller inject humor into their voices. They are warm and likable—you trust them. They get particular voice-over parts because of the quality of their voices.

Each voice has built-in characteristics that allow the person a broad range of age and emotions. Deborah Gear proclaims, "I would defy anyone to listen to my tape and guess how old I really am." Your natural voice can serve you well. It's what you do with your voice that really counts.

What Are the Spots That Use Voice-Overs?

The type of spots called for include spokespersons, commercial characters, promos (promotionals), informationals (for industrials and religious markets), phone patches (professionally recorded phone messages), and animated characters (supplying voice-overs for cartoon characters and inanimate objects).

Preparing Your Voice for the Job

The job of the voice-over performer is to sell a product. Charles Cowing says, "Selling a product is the only job; it's being able to lend your emotions to a bar of soap." Therefore, as with on-camera commercials, you must understand the copy and be able to read it smoothly and sound believable. Your listeners will not respond to your recommendations unless they trust your voice.

Begin to practice by listening. Put on your radio or television. If it's television, close your eyes and listen to the voice (watching someone speaking the words is entirely different from just listening). Note how they shade the words. Pay attention to the texture and tone, observe how they ask a question, listen for the inflections. Tom Perkins, a recording engineer, says, "I'm terribly sensitive to tone—not what's being said, but *how* it is said. In this business you have to become sensitive to texture and tone." Ellene Faison an actress and voice-over teacher says, "Listen, listen, listen to different voices. Record your own voice . . . listen to it . . . hear yourself . . . practice your voice. Get to know what your speaking voice can do. Your voice should make your audience care and want to know more about the product."

More Tips for Practice

Select copy from radio or television commercials and record it in your own voice on your tape recorder. Don't listen to your voice while you are recording—that's what playbacks are for.

Listen for words you have difficulty in pronouncing and work on them. Pitch is the musical level at which we speak. Raise and lower your pitch. Use it to avoid monotone and to get variety into your voice. To put emphases on a particular word, try

raising the pitch on that word. Increasing and decreasing loud-
ness tends to give the phrase meaning.

A BBC (British Broadcasting Corporation) producer
believes there are four elements in a verbal commercial: voice,
music, sound effects, and silence. A pause can be a powerful
and dramatic addition to your reading—but first, a word of caution: a voice-over pause must never be as long as a regular pause
or else your reading will sound as if it died. It will seem much
longer than a natural pause simply because there's usually nothing else going on at the moment.

For more guidelines on practice copy and voice training, see
the list of books in Appendix D.

Using the Microphone

Tom Perkins has this to say: "Unless your vocal highs and lows
change drastically, stay about six inches to one foot from the
mike. For more intimate copy, get right close to the mike, but
be careful to avoid "popping *p*'s" or any consonant or sound
that is a blast of air. The mike will pick it up, and it's very
unpleasant."

How to Control the "Poppings" Learn how to move your lips
when you say a *p*. Hang a tissue in front of your mouth. Say *p*,
f, *b*, etc. Say the sounds in several different ways. Observe the
tissue movement. Use breath control and mouth control. It's
good to have a strong lung capacity. One word of caution: never
blow into a microphone. This can do a great deal of damage to
the mike. Don't touch the microphone, either; a slight touch
will make it go "boom."

Mouth Noises The microphone is extremely sensitive and will
pick up all sorts of unexpected noises. Dental work, particularly bridgework, is a major offender. The microphone picks up the
clicking noise. Even saliva rolling around in your mouth pro-
duces a loud sound. The microphone is also very sensitive to
what you wear. Jewelry, keys, earrings, loose change—anything
that could possibly make noise—should be either left at home
or kept well out of the microphone's range.

Tom Perkins provides another piece of sound advice: "Don't wear a hat. Sound reflects off the inside band and can cause the voice to sound hard and strident." Another tip from Tom concerns handling paper. Learn to do it quietly, especially when you have a multipage script. Peter Thomas, a well-known voice-over and industrial actor, knows how to pick up a page without making a sound. He slides the page down slowly, puts the sheet quietly onto the next, and never stops reading.

The Demo (Demonstration Tape)

What your headshot is to on-camera work, your demo is to voice-over work. This tape represents the best work you do. It should be no longer than two minutes. If the agents are not interested in the first five seconds, they're not going to listen to the rest of it. You must catch them in the first five or six seconds.

If you do characters, they should last no longer than it takes to establish them. This can range from a tag (a short line that usually ends a spot) or a twenty-second commercial. For your natural voice, use four or five spots. Include changes in your emotional attitude. Inject humor, show high energy, be quiet and intimate, sound authoritative, be dramatic, and so on. Just do it well and make it short.

As for copy, it's up to you whether you use actual copy, create original material, or, like some actors, choose to use a little of both. In general, it is okay to use material that has been written and recorded by someone else for a real product or company—as long as you use the material for your demo tape only. Make sure the copy suits your voice and that you have the presentation down pat.

A professional demo tape is made in a recording studio. The studio will provide the background and sound effects. Generally, the charge is about $250 an hour. You pay for the recording session, which might take an hour, and the time it takes for the mix (insertion of background, music, etc.), which generally takes about two hours. The average total is $750, but you should shop around. Different areas and different studios vary in cost.

Marketing Yourself for Voice-Over Work

Agents should always be part of your mailing list. However, the door isn't always ajar for newcomers, especially in the major markets. But, you never know. Charles Cowing says, "There will always be room for voice-over people who know how to sell."

According to several voice-over performers, there is tons of union and nonunion work out there. By marketing yourself, you are free to contact recording studios, producers, and advertising agencies.

An excellent source for your voice-over mailing list is a book called *The Standard Directory of Advertising Agencies*, which can be found in most libraries. You will find that some top agencies have media budgets of over twenty-five million dollars. Many more have budgets between ten and twenty million dollars.

Actors in the field suggest that you target your list to those agencies that have a three-million-dollar budget in bookings. These agencies generally don't have the allocated funds to go through voice-over agencies, so they book their talent directly. I found eight hundred pages of names of agencies throughout the country who fit into the above category. Call each one and say, "I do voice-overs." Ask for the casting person, and ask if you may send them your tape. Deborah Gear says, "That's how I'm getting there."

Cable Television

At this writing, a very exciting opportunity is being developed for senior performers. Cable networks are currently being created and will be distributed through cable systems, direct broadcast, satellites, and over-the-air broadcast facilities presenting programming directed to the fifty-plus population. These networks plan on providing programs for the more than 65 million Americans who are fifty years of age and older. Additionally, they plan to develop working relationships with national advertisers who manufacture products and/or provide services directed to the fifty-plus market. As a result, this will create a strong advertising base targeted at the fifty-plus population, which in turn should result in lucrative jobs for mature actors for commercials as well as other areas.

Another piece of good news is that these networks are committed to working with personnel over fifty. Retirees are encouraged to rejoin the work force—to use the expertise they gathered over the years to become a part of the network. This includes on-air talent as well as other areas of the performing arts.

A Few Facts About Cable Television and the Market

1. Cable television continues to grow, with over 63 percent of all households currently subscribing to more than 11,000 cable systems throughout the United States. These subscribers include forty million adults over the age of fifty.
2. Direct Broadcast Satellites (DBS) and the anticipated arrival of interactive television will bring new dimensions to the viewer, whose viewing choices will continue to grow dramatically into the next century.
3. The fifty-plus market represents 40 percent of total consumer demand, 50 percent of all disposable income, 70 percent of United States wealth, and 77 percent of total financial assets. Clearly, financially secure seniors control an enormous amount of accumulated wealth.
4. The fifty-plus segment of the population has more than 65 million active, vital individuals who represent a nine-hundred-billion-dollar-plus market that continues to expand.

New opportunities are developing daily. Watch for them, and be ready for those that promise to provide a gainful addition to your second career!

Appendix A

Practice Commercial Copy

I have written the following commercial copy using the names of products and companies that, to the best of my knowledge, are all fictitious. If any contain existing copy or the names of actual products or companies, my use of them was unintentional and coincidental.

Doonsbury Figure Tarts

Keeping my weight down would be easy if it weren't for my passion for goodies. I can't resist sweets. That's why I love Doonsbury Figure Tarts. It's like eating your way to heaven. Figure Tarts are so chunky-delicious you can't believe they're a diet sweet with only one hundred calories per bar. If you love sweets and can't keep your weight down, satisfy your sweet tooth . . . with Doonsbury Figure Tarts.

Security Savings Bank

At some banks, looking good and smiling may be all you need to be a good teller. At Security Savings, a teller must know much more. Our tellers must be able to help the customer with different types of checking accounts, information on savings, new ways to save money, and a whole lot more. Wouldn't you rather have a teller who thinks of you and your money? Security—the bank that lets you sleep at night.

Arcorub

If you suffer from back pain, just think of being able to rub in strong relief right where you hurt. Now, with amazing new Arcorub, you can get strong relief, and it's odorless too. In seconds, Arcorub begins to concentrate tremendous relief directly at the point of minor back pain. Strong relief that lasts for hours, and the remarkable thing is that there are no side effects. New Arcorub. Strong relief right where you hurt.

Buffies Canadian Candies

Not long ago, we country folks had this great secret: Buffies Canadian Candies. After all, we harvested the delicious, juicy fruits for Buffies Canadian fruit flavors. We skimmed the cream and churned the butter to make "buttercream" and other flavors. Then the word spread, and everyone here found out about those delicious crunchy flavors. Now that the secret is out, do you think we can keep Buffies Canadian Candies north of the border?

Delake Vegetable Soup

Life in this valley is busy and hard. But it's an honest life. I believe in good things . . . in doing right for my family. There's a good many soups out there, but not like Delake Vegetable Soup. It's got honest and wholesome taste. Real zesty flavor. A natural combination of fresh vegetables that makes your mouth water. Delake Vegetable Soup: the only soup that really satisfies.

Endit's Cough Syrup

We take care of each other. So when I have a cough, my husband can't do enough for me. He buys cold capsules, aspirin, nasal drops, decongestants. He doesn't know that Endit's Cough Syrup has all of these ingredients in one bottle.

Endit's Cough Syrup. It contains nasal drops, aspirin, cold capsules, and decongestant to relieve the cough and take away the pain. So when I have a cough, I take Endit's Cough Syrup for relief and a heavenly night's rest.

Lonadventure Credit Card

I don't like to carry cash, and I often had problems cashing my personal check. Then I discovered the Lonadventure Credit Card. This turned out to be my best investment. Not only do I take the whole family out to dinner on birthdays and special occasions, but I get discounts on 50 percent of my shopping needs and a really low interest charge. Lonadventure Credit Card. There's no better card in the world.

Nettime Car Phone

I'm just passionate about driving in the country. I like the peace and quiet. I love the smell of the flowers and shrubs. I enjoy visiting antique shops and auctions and discovering new roads, and sometimes I just like to drive.

The trouble is, my children worry about me. They think just because I'm older, I can't do the things I've done most of my life. So they gave me a Nettime Car Phone for Christmas. I never thought I'd use it. And you know what? Not only do I enjoy calling them, but running out of gas or getting a flat tire are never problems anymore. One phone call on my Nettime Car Phone and help comes right away. How did I every drive without it? Nettime Car Phone. It's a must for everyone.

Windsor Health Plan

When I go to a doctor—and believe me, I've been often enough—I want a topnotch physician who cares about me and my problems. I want to be treated like a human being, not just a number.

Well, Windsor Health has come up with the answer. They have topnotch board-certified doctors whom they have selected for their skills and caring attitude. They have access to over two hundred hospitals and a worldwide emergency care plan. Windsor Health Plan. Their only concern is you. Who could ask for anything more.

Marking Copy

Marking copy is adding a series of notations that enables you to read copy consistently and with proper emphasis. It also helps you prepare for better delivery. If you have trouble reading the copy the same way each time, the markings will help train you to be conscious of the techniques you are employing.

The Marks

Emphasis	Underline the word or words
Color and key words	Circle the word, words, or phrase
Unique selling point	Bracket the phrase [ ]
Pauses	Double slant //
Inflections	An upward mark for high inflection ∧

Let's take another look at the Arcorub commercial copy. Copy the words onto a clean sheet of paper. Then underline the emphasized words, which are the root words that convey meaning: *suffer, back pain, strong relief, can get, odorless, concentrate, relief.* Circle the color and key words, which color the copy: *Arcorub, amazing, rub in, tremendous relief.* The sponsor's name is a color and key word. Always say it with love and affection.

Bracket the unique selling point, which includes the words that make this product different or better: *strong relief right where you hurt.*

Use a double slant for pauses, which are used to call attention to a word or statement. *Strong relief that lasts for hours //.*

Mark the inflections, which break the monotony of the voice: *Amazing, strong relief, remarkable, tremendous.*

If you make every mark that I have suggested, the copy might get to look like chicken scratches. However, when you practice at home, begin by using all the marks. As you establish your techniques, you will find that you will only require some of the marks.

Of course, you may invent your own system. The marks you use can be quite individual. You may use any symbols that make you comfortable. The bottom line is to develop a system that is consistent. If a circle means *color* and *key* one time, it must mean *color* and *key* every time, and so on.

For practice, duplicate the commercial copy in the beginning of this appendix and mark away!

Appendix B
Listing of Agents and Casting Directors

Following are a selected list of agents and casting directors. They can be found in a wide variety of trade papers, books, and other publications and recommendations. At the time of this writing, these lists are current. However, due to the nature of the business, changes do occur. Check with your SAG branch office and local trade publications monthly for current updates.

Atlanta, GA

Atlanta Model and Talent, Inc., 3030 Peachtree Road NW, Atlanta, GA 30305
(404) 261-9627

People's Store, 1776 Peachtree Road NW, Atlanta, GA 30309
(404) 874-6448

Serendipity Models International Inc., 550 Pharr Road, Atlanta, GA 30305
(404) 237-4040

Boston, MA

Chute, 115 Newbury Street, Boston, MA 02116
(617) 262-2626

Lordly and Dame, Inc., 51 Church Street, Boston, MA 02116
(617) 482-3593

Maggie Inc., 35 Newbury Street, Boston, MA 02116
(617) 536-2639

Elle, 376 North Street, Boston, MA 02113
(617) 523-2100

Collinge Pickman, 138 Mt. Auburn Street,
Cambridge, MA 02138
(617) 492-4212

Chicago, IL

Alderman Casting, 190 N. State Street, Chicago, IL 60601
(312) 839-4250

Chicago Model and Talent Management, 435 N. LaSalle
Street, Chicago, IL 60610
(312) 527-2977

David Lee Talent Group, 70 W. Hubbard Street Suite 200,
Chicago, IL 60610
(312) 670-4444

Susanne Johnson, 108 W. Oak Street, Chicago, IL 60610
(312) 943-8375

Cherie Mann Casting, 1540 N. LaSalle Street,
Chicago, IL 60610
(312) 751-2927

Dallas, TX

Shirley Abrams Casting Inc., P. O. Box 29199,
Dallas, TX 75229
(214) 484-6774

Cambell Agency, 3903 Lemmon Avenue, Dallas, TX 75219
(214) 522-8991

Mary Collins, 5956 Sherry Lane, Dallas, TX 75225
(214) 360-0900

Elan M/T Mgmt., 13601 Preston Road, Dallas, TX 75240
(214) 239-2398

J&D Talent, Inc., 1825 Market Ctr. Blvd., Dallas, TX 75207
(214) 239-2398

Margo Manning Casting, 11126 Shady Trail,
Dallas, TX 75229
(214) 869-2323

Los Angeles, CA

A Special Talent Agency, 6253 Hollywood Blvd., Los
Angeles, CA, 90628
(213) 467-7068

Agency for Performing Arts, 9000 Sunset Blvd.,
Los Angeles CA 90669
(213) 273-0744

Applegate 7 Associates, 1633 Vista del Mar,
Los Angeles, CA 90028
(213) 461-2726

Bobby Ball Talent Agency, 8484 Wilshire Blvd.,
Beverly Hills, CA 90211
(213) 852-1357

Terry Berland Casting, 12166 West Olympic Blvd.,
Los Angeles, CA 90064
(310) 571-4141

Nina Blanchard, 1717 North Highland Avenue,
Los Angeles, CA 90628
(213) 462-7341

Brown/West Casting, 7319 Beverly Blvd.,
Los Angeles, CA 90036
(213) 938-2575

Iris Button, 1450 Belfast Drive, Los Angeles, CA 90669
(213) 652-0954

Cast & Crew, 4201 West Burbank Street, Burbank, CA 91505
(818) 848-0906

Colours, 7551 Melrose Avenue, Los Angeles, CA 90046
(213) 658-7072

Mary Webb Davis Agency, 515 N. La Cienega Blvd., Los
Angeles, CA 90048
(213) 655-6747

Gilla Roos Ltd., 9744 Wilshire Blvd.,
Beverly Hills, CA 90212
(310) 274-9356

Special Artists Agency, 335 North Maple Drive,
Beverly Hills, CA 90210
(310) 859-9688

Gilda Stratton, 4000 Warner Blvd., Burbank, CA 91522
(818) 954-2843

Tepper & Gallegos, 611 North Larchmont Blvd.,
Burbank, CA 90004
(213) 469-3577

Miami and Fort Lauderdale, FL

Act 1 Model & Talent Agency, 1205 Washington Avenue,
Miami Beach, FL 33139
(305) 672-0200

Aaron Models, 2803 East Commercial Blvd.,
Ft. Lauderdale, FL 33308
(305) 772-8944

Avenue Productions Inc., 3405 North Federal Highway,
Ft. Lauderdale, FL 33306
(305) 561-1226

Central Casting of Florida, 10 NE 11th Avenue,
Ft. Lauderdale, FL 33301 (Attn: Enid Polan Howell)
(305) 525-8351

David & Lee Miami, 820 Ocean Drive,
Miami Beach, FL 33139
(305) 538-5191

Green & Green, 1688 Meridian Avenue,
Miami Beach, FL 33139
(305) 532-9880

Models Exchange, 2425 East Commercial Blvd.,
Ft. Lauderdale, FL 33308 (Attn: Jeffrey Koslow)
(305) 491-1014

Plus Models, 1400 Ocean Drive, South Miami, FL 33139
(305) 672-9882

Michele Pommier Models, Inc., 81 Washington Avenue,
Miami Beach, FL 33139 (Attn: Sherry Lynn)
(305) 672-9344

Scott Harvey Model & Talent Management Agency,
2734 East Oakland Park Blvd., Ft. Lauderdale, FL 33306
(305) 565-1211

Minneapolis and St. Paul, MN

Creative Casting, 10 South 5th Street,
Minneapolis, MN 55402
(612) 375-0525

Kimberly Franson Agency, 4620 West 77th Street,
Minneapolis, MN 55435
(612) 830-0111

Models Resource Center, 27 North 4th Street,
Minneapolis, MN 55401
(612) 339-2441

Eleanor Moore Model & Talent Agency, Inc.,
1610 West Lake Street, Minneapolis, MN 55408
(612) 827-3823

New York, New York

Michael Amato Agency, 1650 Broadway,
New York, NY 10019
(212) 247-4456

Peter Beilin Agency, 230 Park Avenue, New York, NY 10169
(212) 949-9119

Bookers, Inc., 150 Fifth Avenue, New York, NY 10011
(212) 645-9706

Jane Brinker Casting Ltd., 51 West 16th Street,
New York, NY 10011
(212) 924-3322

Donald Case Casting Inc., 386 Park Avenue South,
New York, NY 10016
(212) 889-6555

Merry L. Delmonte Casting & Productions, Inc., 555 West
57th Street (CBS Broadcast Center), New York, NY 10019
(212) 757-9838

Donna De Seta Casting (ICDA), 525 Broadway,
New York, NY 10012 (Indicate "extra work" on photo)
(212) 274-9696

Sylvia Fay, 71 Park Avenue, New York, NY 10016

Ford Classic Women, 344 East 59th Street,
New York, NY 10022
(212) 688-0007

Maureen Fremont Casting, 1001 Sixth Avenue,
New York, NY 10016
(212) 302-1215

FunnyFace Today, 151 East 31st Street, New York, NY 10016
(212) 686-4343

Gonzalez Model & Talent, 112 East 23rd Street,
New York, NY 10010
(212) 982-5626

Hyde-Hamlet Casting, Times Square Station, Box 884,
New York, NY 10108 (Attn: Sarah Hyde-Hamlet)
(718) 783-9634

Kee Casting, 511 Avenue of the Americas,
New York, NY 10011
(212) 995-0794

Jodi Kipperman Casts, 39 West 19th Street,
New York, NY 10011
(212) 627-5551

Liz Lewis Casting Partners, 3 West 18th Street,
New York, NY 10011
(212) 645-1500

Debbee May Agency, 79 Barrow Street, New York, NY 10014
(212) 633-9821

McDonald/Richards, Inc., 156 Fifth Avenue,
New York, NY 10010
(212) 627-3100

Navarro/Bertoni & Assoc., 101 West 31st Street,
New York, NY 10001
(212) 736-9272

Nouvelle Talent Inc., 20 Bethune Street,
New York, NY 10014
(212) 645-0940

Oppenheim-Christie Associates, Ltd., 13 East 37th Street,
New York, NY 10016
(212) 213-4330

Fifi Oscard Agency, Inc., 24 West 40th Street,
New York, NY 10018
(212) 764-1100

Dorothy Palmer Talent Agency Inc., 235 West 56th Street,
New York, NY 10019
(212) 765-4280

Scott Powers Productions, Inc., 150 Fifth Avenue,
New York, NY 10011
(212) 242-4700

Plus Models Management, 49 West 37th Street,
New York, NY 10018
(212) 997-1785

R&L Model & Talent Management, 645 Fifth Avenue,
6th Floor, New York, NY 10019
(212) 935-2300

Gilla Roos Ltd., 16 West 22nd Street, New York, NY 10010
(Attn: David Roos)
(212) 727-7820

Schiffman, Ekman, Morrison & Marx, Inc.,
22 West 19th Street, New York, NY 10011
(212) 627-5500

William Schill Agency Inc., 250 West 57th Street,
New York, NY 10019
(212) 315-5919

Joy Weber Casting, 250 West 57th Street,
New York, NY 10019
(212) 245-5220

Wilfley-Todd Casting, 60 Madison Avenue,
New York, NY 10010
(212) 685-3537

Van Der Veer People, Inc. 400 East 57th Street,
New York, NY 10022
(212) 688-2880

Philadelphia, PA

Askins Models, Newmarket Headhouse Square #200,
Philadelphia, PA 19147
(215) 925-7795.

Expressions Agency, 104 Church Street,
Philadelphia, PA 19106
(215) 923-4420

Hedges May Casting, 1627 Walnut Street,
Philadelphia, PA 19103
(800) 331-7840

Mike Lemon Casting, Callowhill Office Center,
413 North 7th Street, Philadelphia, PA 19123
(215) 627-8927

The Philadelphia Casting Co. Inc., 128 Chestnut Street,
Philadelphia, PA 19106
(215) 592-7577

Reinhard Model & Talent Agency, 2021 Arch Street,
Philadelphia, PA 10103
(215) 567-2008

Phoenix, AZ

Dom's Agency, One East Camelback Road,
Phoenix, AZ 85012
(602) 263-1918

Leighton Model & Talent Agency, 3333 North 44th Street,
Phoenix, AZ 85018
(602) 224-9255

Premier Talent, 4603 North 16th Street, Phoenix, AZ 85016
(602) 468-1292

Tor/Ann Talent & Booking, 6711 North 21st Street,
Phoenix, AZ
(602) 263-8708

San Francisco, CA

Avalon Models, 166 Geary Street, San Francisco, CA 94108
(415) 421-8211

Casting Works, Inc., 1045 Sansome Street,
San Francisco, CA 94111
(415) 922-6218

Demeter & Reed Ltd. Agency, 70 Zoe Street,
San Francisco, CA 94107
(415) 777-1337

Look Model Agency, 166 Geary Street,
San Francisco, CA 94108
(415) 781-2822

Perseus Model & Talent, 369 Pine Street,
San Francisco, CA 94104
(415) 543-9049

Seattle, WA

Actors Group, 291 First Avenue S., Seattle, WA 98121
(206) 624-9465

Chastain & Company Talent, 14 Alaska Way S.,
Seattle, WA 98104
(206) 233-1497

Lola Hallowell Agency, 1700 Westlake Avenue N.,
Seattle, WA 98109
(206) 281-4646

Washington, DC (Maryland, Virginia)

BHK Arts Consultants, 326 N Street S.W.,
Washington, DC 20024
(202) 554-0131

Central Casting, 2229 N. Charles Street,
Baltimore, MD 21218
(301) 889-3200

Central Casting, 623 Pennsylvania Avenue S.E.,
Washington, DC 20003
(202) 547-6300

Model Store, 1529 Wisconsin Avenue,
Washington, DC 20007
(202) 333-3560

Nova Modeling, 206 Liberty Street, Baltimore, MD 21202
(410) 753-6682

Taylor Royal Agency, 2308 South Road,
Baltimore, MD 21209
(301) 466-5959

The Artist Agency, 3076 M Street N.W.,
Washington, DC 20007
(202) 342-0933

Appendix C
SAG/AFTRA Branch Offices

Arizona
SAG & AFTRA
1616 East Indian School Road #330
Phoenix, AZ 85016
(602) 265-2712

Atlanta
SAG & AFTRA
455 East Paces Ferry Road NE Suite #334
Atlanta, GA 30305
(404) 239-0131

Boston*
SAG & AFTRA
11 Beacon Street #513
Boston, MA 02108
(617) 742-2688

Chicago
SAG & AFTRA
75 East Wacker Drive, 14th Floor
Chicago, IL 60601
(312) 372-8081

---

*The Boston office is a regional office that also covers Maine, New Hampshire, Vermont, Massachusetts, and part of Connecticut.

Cincinnati/Columbus/Dayton/Louisville
AFTRA
1814–16 Carew Tower
Cincinnati, OH 45202
(513) 579-8668

Cleveland
SAG & AFTRA
1367 East 6th Street #229
Cleveland, OH 44114
(216) 579-9035

Dallas/Ft. Worth
SAG & AFTRA
6060 North Central Expressway #302-LB 604
Dallas, TX 75206
(214) 363-8300

Denver*
AFTRA
950 South Cherry Street #502
Denver, CO 80222
(303) 757-6226

Detroit
SAG & AFTRA
28690 Southfield Road 290 A & B
Lanthrup Village, MI 48076
(313) 559-9540

Fresno
AFTRA
PO Box 11961
Fresno, CA 93776
(209) 222-7065

---

*The Denver office is a regional office that also covers Nevada, New Mexico, and Utah.

Hawaii
SAG & AFTRA
949 Kapiolani Boulevard #105
Honolulu, HI 96814
(808) 538-6122

Houston
SAG & AFTRA
2650 Foutainview #326
Houston, TX 77057
(713) 972-1806

Kansas City
AFTRA
PO Box 32162
4000 Baltimore, 2nd Floor
Kansas City, MO 64111
(816) 753-4557

Los Angeles
SAG
7065 Hollywood Boulevard
Hollywood, CA 90028
(213) 465-4600

AFTRA
6922 Hollywood Boulevard
Hollywood, CA 90028
(213) 461-8111

Miami*
SAG
300 North Kendall Drive #620
Miami, FL 33156
(305) 670-7677

---

*The Miami office is a regional office that also covers Alabama, Arkansas, Louisiana, Mississippi, North Carolina, South Carolina, South Virginia, and West Virginia.

AFTRA
20401 NW 2nd Avenue #102
Miami, FL 33169
(305) 652-4824

Minneapolis/St. Paul
SAG & AFTRA
15 South 9th Street #400
Minneapolis, MN 55404
(612) 371-9120

Nashville
SAG & AFTRA
1108 17th Avenue South
Nashville, TN 37212
(615) 327-2958 (SAG)
(615) 327-2944 (AFTRA)

New Orleans
AFTRA
2475 Canal Street #108
New Orleans, LA 70119
(504) 822-6568

New York
SAG
1515 Broadway, 44th Floor
New York, NY 10036
(212) 944-1030

AFTRA
260 Madison Avenue, 7th Floor
New York, NY 10016
(212) 532-0800

Omaha
AFTRA
3000 Farnham Street #3 East
Omaha, NE 68131
(402) 346-8384

Orlando
AFTRA
Major Building
5728 Major Boulevard #264
Orlando, FL 32819
(407) 354-2230

Peoria
AFTRA
2907 Springfield Road
East Peoria, IL 61611
(309) 699-5052

Philadelphia
SAG & AFTRA
230 South Broad Street, 10th Floor
Philadelphia, PA 19102
(215) 545-3150 (SAG)
(215) 732-0507 (AFTRA)

Pittsburgh
AFTRA
625 Stanwix Street
The Penthouse
Pittsburgh, PA 15222
(412) 281-6767

Portland
AFTRA
516 SE Morrison #M-3
Portland, OR 97214
(503) 238-6914

Rochester
AFTRA
1600 Crossroads Office Building
Rochester, NY 14614
(716) 232-3730

Sacramento/Stockton
AFTRA
836 Garnet Street
West Sacramento, CA 95691
(916) 372-1966

St. Louis
SAG & AFTRA
906 Olive Street #1006
St. Louis, MO 63101
(314) 231-8410

San Diego
SAG & AFTRA
7827 Convoy Court #400
San Diego, CA 92111
(619) 278-7695

San Francisco
SAG & AFTRA
235 Pine Street, 11th Floor
San Francisco, CA 94104
(415) 391-7510

Schenectady
AFTRA
170 Ray Avenue
Schenectady, NY 12304
(518) 381-4836

Seattle
SAG & AFTRA
601 Valley Street #200
Seattle, WA 98109
(206) 282-2506

Stamford
AFTRA
100 Prospect Street
Stamford, CT 06901
(203) 348-1308

Tri-State (includes Cincinnati, Columbus & Dayton, OH; Indianapolis, IN & Louisville, KY)
AFTRA
128 East 6th Street #802
Cincinnati, OH 45202
(513) 579-8668

Washington, DC/Maryland/Virginia
SAG
The Highland House
5480 Wisconsin Avenue #201
Chevy Chase, MD 20815
(301) 657-2560

AFTRA
4340 East West Highway #204
Bethesda, MD 20814
(301) 657-2560

Appendix D
Recommended Reading

Acting Guides

Bernard, Jan. 1993. *Film and Television Acting*. Newton, MA: Focal Press.

Colyer, Carlton. 1989. *The Art of Acting*. Colorado Springs, CO: Meriwether Publishing Ltd.

Harmon, Renee. 1984. *The Actor's Survival Guide for Today's Film Industry*. Englewood Cliffs, NJ: Prentice Hall Inc.

Henry, Mari Lyn, and Lynne Rogers. 1994. *How to Be a Working Actor: The Inside Guide to Finding Jobs in Theater, Film, and Television*. New York: Watson Guptell Publications.

Commercials

Carr, Kate. 1982. *How You Can Star in TV Commercials: Your Kids, Cat and Grandparents Too*. New York: Rawson, Wade.

Dougan, Pat. 1995. *Professional Acting in Television Commercials: Techniques, Exercises, Copy, and Storyboards*. Portsmouth, NH: Heinemann.

Fridell, Squire. 1986. *Acting in Television Commercials for Fun and Profit*. New York: Crown Trade Paperbacks.

Hunt, Cecely. 1982. *How to Get Work and Make Money in Commercials and Modeling*. New York: Van Nostrand Reinhold.

Johnson-Watson, Vernee. 1994. *Commercials Just My Speed*. Sylmar, CA: Wizards Production Group.

See, Joan. 1993 *Acting in Commercials: A Guide to Auditioning and Performing on Camera*. New York: Backstage Books.

Voice-Overs and Industrials

Bareiss, Peter, and Martha Porter. 1991. *Off the Air: A Collection of Lively Voice-Over Scripts for a Memorable Demo.* Chicago: Chicago Play Inc.

Blu, Susan, and Molly Ann Mullen. 1992. *Word of Mouth: A Guide to Commercial Voice-Over Excellence.* Universal City, CA: Pomegranate Press Ltd.

Cronauer, Adrian. 1990. *How to Read Copy.* Chicago: Bonus Books Inc.

Linklater, Kristin. 1976. *Freeing the Natural Voice.* New York: Drama Book Publishers.

Marrs, Carol. 1992. *The Complete Book of Speech Communication: Workbook of Ideas and Activities for Students of Speech and Theater.* Colorado Springs, CO: Meriwether Publishing Ltd.

McCallion, Mitchall. 1988. *The Voice Book: For Actors, Public Speakers, and Everyone Who Wants to Make the Most of Their Voice.* New York: Theater Arts Books/Routledge.

The Standard Directory of Advertising Agencies. 1996. New Providence, NJ: National Register Publishing.

Steele, William Paul. 1994. *Acting in Industrials: The Business of Acting for Business.* Portsmouth, NH: Heinemann

Whitfields, Alice. 1992. *Take It from the Top: How to Earn Your Living in Radio, Television and Voice-Over.* New York: Ring-U-Turkey Press.

Modeling

Balhorn, Linda. 1990. *Professional Model's Handbook.* Albany, NY: Milady Publishing Co.

Harman, Tori, and Carolyn Strauss. 1988. *Specialty Modeling.* New York: Dutton.

Perkins, Eric. 1985. *The Insider's Guide to Modeling.* New York: Nautilus Books Inc.

Appendix E

Glossary

The following are words and phrases used in the field. Being familiar with them will give you an edge and add to your professionalism.

Action: The command given by the director to start a scene or any business or movement by the players.

AD: An AD (assistant director) signs you in and out, tells you when to go to lunch, notifies you when you need to get make-up and wardrobe, assigns your call time, and answers just about any question you might have. The AD can be a great help on the set.

Age range: Ages that an actor can possibly portray.

Agency: Either a model/talent agency or an advertising agency. The former handles the actor/model and the latter prepares advertising for clients (which involves creating and producing print ads, television commercials, or promotions).

Audition: A tryout for a film, commercial, etc., which is generally conducted by a casting director.

Background: Another term for *extra*.

Better Business Bureau: A clearinghouse for individuals with questions about the legitimacy and practices of businesses.

Booking: An offer of employment for a specific job on a specific day. If you (or your agent) verbally accepts, it is regarded as a binding agreement.

Buyout: An agreed-to advance of full payment to a performer.

Callback: A request for you to go back for another audition. It means you seemed right for the job and could get it.

Camera-ready: When you are told to come camera-ready, it means you are to report for a shoot with your makeup on, ready to work.

Casting director: The person responsible for finding the right performer for a production, commercial, etc.

CDI: Compact Disk Interactive. Computer-compatible disk used in consumer products.

CD-ROM: Compact Disk–Read Only Memory. Computer-compatible disk capable of reproducing full-motion video.

Cheat to camera: To slightly turn your face to the camera so as to show more of your face.

Client: The person who pays to have the commercial or ad made.

Cold reading: Reading copy for the first time. The actor is given very little, if any, rehearsal time before performing.

Composite: The business card of the working model. Generally a 5" x 7" card showing a model in various poses to give the potential client an idea of the photographability of the performer. Pertinent information (name, measurements, age range, etc.) is included.

Contact sheet: A photographic print sheet made up of all the shots from a roll of film used to determine which photos are to be used and, therefore, enlarged.

Copy: The text of a commercial. Also called a script.

Cut: When one scene is abruptly changed to the next.

CU: Close-up.

Cue card: A card set up near the camera to help you remember your lines.

Day rate: The fee a model receives for a day's booking.

Demo: A demonstration tape of your best work. A sales tool used for agents, casting people, and producers. Also used for voice-overs.

Flat rate: The fee for a booking regardless of how long it takes.

Freelance: An actor who works through more than one agency rather than signing exclusive contracts.

Go-see: An appointment for a photographer to view models for a prospective job.

Headshot: Usually an 8" x 10" black-and-white photograph. The headshot is the actor's calling card.

Hero: The product

Industrial: A film or live production for promotion. It may be an educational, sales, or instructional film, but not a commercial film meant for general release.

Inflection: The raising or lowering of the pitch of your voice.

Location: The site of a shoot out of the studio, either indoors or outdoors.

Logo: A communication to the public via an image.

MOS: Without sound (stands for *mit out sound*).

Pops: Noises resulting from hard consonants spoken directly into the mike.

Production company: The company that was hired to shoot the commercial.

Promo: A promotional spot. It promotes a product or, more often, a service.

Residuals: The money paid for rerunning a commercial.

Rhythm: The cadence of the speaking voice.

Scale wage: Minimum wage as designated by the unions.

Session fee: The money you are paid for the initial day's work on a commercial.

SFX: Sound effects

Shoot: Industry's jargon for filming or taping.

Slate: Identifying yourself on camera before you begin the audition. When the cameraperson says "slate," say your name directly to the camera.

Storyboard: A series of cartoonlike drawings outlining the shots required for a television commercial or print ad. It is combined with a story guideline.

Tag(s): Short one or two lines of copy that either end a spot or stand alone to identify and describe a product.

Take: A single attempt to record a shot on camera.

Talent: Any actor who is employed as a principal. This term has no correlation with whether or not you have any.

Tear sheet: The pages from a publication in which a model has appeared. The model collects these for his or her portfolio.

Tone: The sound quality of the voice (sexy, nasal, strident, etc.).

Upgrade: To move from the ranks of an extra in a commercial or film to a speaking part.

Voucher: After doing a job, the model should get a three-copy receipt (furnished by the model's agency) signed by the client showing the hours worked and the total charge. The client gets a copy, the agency gets a copy, and the model keeps a copy.

Wrap: The last shot of the day. Everyone can go home.